Angel
of the
Amazon

THE STORY OF DR. BILL WOODS OBE

~ AS TOLD BY ~

VICTOR MAXWELL

AMBASSADOR

BELFAST ◆ **GREENVILLE**
NORTHERN IRELAND   SOUTH CAROLINA

Angel of the Amazon

© Copyright 1997 Victor Maxwell

ISBN 1 84030 004 3

AMBASSADOR PRODUCTIONS LTD,
Providence House
16 Hillview Avenue,
Belfast, BT5 6JR
Northern Ireland

Emerald House,
1 Chick Springs Road, Suite 206
Greenville,
South Carolina 29609
United States of America

Contents

❖

Introduction

❖

Would you be surprised if I told you it has taken forty years to write this book? That is the length of time I have known Bill Woods and at close hand witnessed this amazing story. In the course of those years we have been members of the same church, trained at the same College and have been working together as colleagues in Acre Gospel Mission.

During this time we have been impressed to see Bill's life shaped by God's hand and the same hand guide his pathway. Thousands have benefited from his single-minded dedication while others have been challenged by his tenacity. From many who have prayed and supported Bill and have followed with genuine interest the amazing development of his life and work has come the demand to write this book.

Bill, somewhat shy and extremely evasive when it comes to speaking of himself and his work, was not easily convinced that the story should be told. To extract the necessary details from him for the book was like taking water out of the proverbial stone. Finally, if not fully persuaded, Bill consented to furnish some information. To gather the other facts and data I had to depend on colleagues and many friends in various professions on different continents. They have all been as enthusiastic as we are and willingly made their contribution to help tell this amazing story.

My sincere thanks to Nina Woods, Bill's sister who kindly recalled many of his early days; Dr. Leia, Bill's right hand in the Leprosy Programme in Acre who was and still is so enthusiastic in her support of Bill; Nurse Rute, Bill's loyal team member who has accompanied all the success of the work in Acre; Senator Flaviano Melo who on several occasions has spoken eloquently of the Leprosy Team in the Brazilian Senate and given his utmost support to it; Dr. Antonio Farias and Pastor Dr. Francisco Poderoso who recalled their experiences with Bill through hard times in Manaus; Bill's good friend Antonio Sampaio who recounted how he benefited from Bill's kindness when he was a poor boy at school in Manaus; the staff at the Alfreda da Mata clinic in Manaus who hold Bill in very high esteem; the friends at the American Leprosy Mission in Greenville, SC, USA, for the data supplied; Sam Lowry of Ambassador Productions for his invitation and encouragement to write the book; to many friends for their various suggestions and finally to my son-in-law Tom and daughter Heather Knutson for their hard work in editing the final manuscript.

If life is 'like a tale that is told' as declared in the Scriptures we readily admit some of those tales are more remarkable than others. Without question Bill Woods' story is an outstanding tale.

Victor Maxwell

Chapter One

Dr. Bill and the Master's Touch

❖

ven though it was still relatively early in the day, the tropical
sun was high enough and hot enough to make the temperatures inside our Volkswagen Kombi rise to uncomfortable
degrees. All the windows were open to catch any breeze as we
negotiated our way over the bumpy road which was made even more
hazardous by gaping potholes at unexpected intervals.

Dr. Bill Woods and I were making our way out of the sprawling
city of Manaus en route to a hospital appointment at the Colonia
Antonio Aleixo. On either side of the road were high concrete apartment blocks and freshly painted brick houses in relatively modern
developments. These new housing estates indicated the growing
prosperity of the great city of Manaus, the capital of Amazonas.
However, in distinct contrast, not even the sunshine could improve
the squalid appearance of many hurriedly erected shanty dwellings
made of cardboard boxes, pieces of wood and plastic sheets. These
shanty towns were springing up around the city and reminded us of
the endemic poverty that so readily co-exists alongside the growing
prosperity in Brazil.

There were no other passengers on board, but in the rear of the Kombi we had several cases which contained Dr. Wood's operating microscope and a variety of surgical instruments which he planned to use once we arrived at the clinic.

In the small talk exchanged we both recalled how this recently improved road used to be a dusty or muddy clay track etched through the forest in the dry season and virtually an impassable quagmire when the rains came. Now we travelled in relative comfort on a black asphalt road even though it was punctuated by unexpected and unannounced pot holes. Once out of town the route was flanked on either side by high banks or deep trenches of red clay. At other times the lush green jungle stood so high it formed a shaded avenue and brought us relief from the hot sun.

The Colonia Antonio Aleixo is a small satellite town about thirty kilometres from Manaus. Originally it was founded as a Colony for the victims of leprosy in the Amazon region. This accounted for its distance from Manaus. In former times the isolated community was a suitable location where society conveniently sent those who suffered from this dreaded and stigmatised disease. Although specialized treatment was available at these colonies, sadly the patients were taken from their families and often sent into forced isolation. There was plenty of heartache and mental anguish. Husbands and wives were separated from each other, and children were deprived of fathers and mothers. Those who were confined indefinitely in these institutions were separated from society and forced to live away from home.

Revolutionary treatment of leprosy had developed in recent years which not only accelerated the healing of leprosy patients but also helped bring a change of attitude toward its victims. Patients could be confidently treated at home without risk to other members of the family. As a result of this change of attitude, the old colony became an opportune location to buy some cheap land to build a house. At the centre of this satellite district of Manaus still stands the Colony's old hospital and clinic which still accommodates some long term patients. Besides the leprosy patients, a greater population of over 50,000 people have now made Colonia Antonio Aleixo their home.

A bit shaken up with the bumpy ride, we came over the brow of a hill and saw stretching out before us irregular rows of small wooden houses on both sides of the road. A few women busied themselves vainly sweeping the red dust from the veranda of their simple homes. While some boys enjoyed the favourite Brazilian pastime - playing soccer, other children, mostly girls, carried tins of water on their heads from a nearby well. Hammocks swung lazily in the shade, and older men rocked to and fro in their wicker chairs. Chickens scampered across the road narrowly missing the wheels of our Kombi which threw up clouds of dust in its wake.

We finally arrived at the small clinic adjacent to the main leprosy hospital and we were glad to ease ourselves out of the vehicle and onto our feet. Bronzed coloured boys dressed only in shorts eagerly gathered round offering to carry our cases in exchange for a few coins.

After we unloaded the equipment I stepped in front of Bill to hold open the front door of the clinic and give him free passage seeing both his arms were full. Just as I went to push the door open someone pulled the same door from the other side. As the door opened a middle aged lady stepped towards us from out of the dark inner corridor. It was clear from her scarred face she bore the tell-tale marks of leprosy. Immediately she recognised Dr. Bill, and her former expressionless and disfigured face suddenly lit up with a radiant smile showing her few white teeth and well worn red gums.

"Dr. Guilherme!" she exclaimed. With that Bill was awkwardly enveloped in her tight embrace as she threw her arms around him and gave him a real bone crushing hug. With a few heavy cases immobilising his arms Bill was an easy prey for this sudden rush of affection.

Somewhat puzzled by the incident I stepped aside so as not to hinder the proceedings and was a little afraid that I would be the next victim of this unknown female's smothering clinch. After the initial and enthusiastic greeting the lady became aware that I was there also. With the same radiant smile still on her face, plus a tear in her eye, she looked at me while pointing at Bill and said, "For me this man is an angel from heaven. I was blind for nine years and he gave me back my sight again. Every day I thank God for sending this man to Brazil."

For two years Dona Joanna had been one of many on a priority waiting list for an operation to remove offending cataracts from her eyes. When her turn finally came there were no beds available at the Getulio Vargas Hospital in Manaus where the delicate surgery was usually performed. To not disappoint the hopeful lady and other eager patients needing similar surgery, Bill made alternative arrangements. Armed with soap, water and disinfectant, he stripped and washed down the walls and floor of the small clinic at Antonio Aleixo and converted it into a makeshift surgical theatre. On the following day he operated on the patients. There was no hospital ward to accommodate them following their operation so each patient was carried back to his home on a stretcher, or as in the case of Dona Joanna, back to the infirmary where she had been interned for two years while awaiting her operation.

Bill Woods is no angel! He would be the first to tell you so. However, inasmuch as an angel is a messenger, for thousands of people in Brazil and beyond, Bill has proved to be God's messenger to bring physical relief to the victims of leprosy. Bill has treated thousands with medication, and he has also dedicated his life and surgical skills to give sight back to more than five hundred people who were previously blinded as a consequence of their disease. He acquired surgical skills and solicited the help of many surgeon friends to perform reconstructive surgery on patients who previously were deformed and left immobile. Many who once were invalids because of their physical deformities now have use of their restored limbs or mechanical aids.

His skills and dedication have given new life to hundreds who were confined to the hidden seclusion of their isolated homes. For those who bore the stigma of all that was associated with the word leprosy, Bill has brought great relief. Couples previously separated from each other and from their families have been reunited and now have the confidence to be happy parents with no need to be separated from their children. Those who in former days were segregated from the public and banished to these purpose built colonies are now able to lead normal lives in their work place and community.

Bill's contribution to the healing of thousands and the improvement of their status in society is all the more astonishing when it is learned that when he first went to Brazil he had no medical skills. He sometimes modestly says that the extent of his knowledge of medicine was limited to what his mother had taught him: "Fenning's Fever Cure does for everything from an ingrown toenail to tonsillitis and on Friday nights take two spoonfuls of Californian Syrup of Figs to keep you regular. If anything goes wrong be sure to take Scott's Emulsion!"

Besides being a dedicated doctor, Bill is a Christian missionary and a keen soul winner. On every opportunity, both in churches and on river journeys to isolated regions of the Amazon, he presents the evangelical message of salvation through Jesus Christ to those who are lost. Only in heaven's register is it recorded how many have trusted the Saviour through Bill's evangelistic preaching and how many saints have benefited from his encouraging medical and spiritual ministry.

Like the boy in the Bible story who gave the Lord his five loaves and two fishes to help feed a hungry multitude, so here again is a story of a life given over to God and the great things God can do with a life wholly yielded to Him. Admittedly, Bill Woods is no angel, but for almost forty years he has been engaged in a work that angels cannot do—namely bringing the Master's touch to the lives and limbs of many victims of this horrendous disease called leprosy.

Chapter Two

Just William

❖

The Albert Bridge spans the River Lagan on the south east side of Belfast, Northern Ireland. From the bridge a series of main arteries fan out leading from the heart of the city to the beautiful rural areas of the Castlereagh Hills and County Down. Among these main thoroughfares are the Ravenhill, Woodstock and Cregagh Roads which box in a tightly packed community with streets of terraced houses and corner-shops.

In a typical street just off the Cregagh Road Mrs. Woods was the proprietor of one of the famous shops that not only sold everything from a needle to an anchor but also made a substantial contribution to the social life of the community in the difficult days of economic depression in the 1930s. In those pre-supermarket days the corner shop opened early in the morning and remained open until late at night for six days every week. It was not only a repository of all that was needed for the local housewife but was often the place where people met and exchanged the local news and gossip.

Mrs. Woods was an industrious and hard working woman, and she was also resourceful and very witty in conversation which marked her out as a favourite character in the community and made her shop a thriving business.

Mr. Woods, with his brother Robert, owned a painting and decorating business in Belfast. The business was abruptly forced to close after a motorcycle accident on the Belfast-to-Bangor road in which Mr. Woods was badly injured and his brother was tragically killed. The trauma of the accident not only terminated the partnership but also left Mr. Woods an invalid for some years.

Another feature of the corner shop was that while business was carried on at the front of the premises, the family lived at the rear of the shop. The oldest of the five Woods children was Nina, the only girl. Unknowingly, the shop would shape her career in future years when she became part of the staff at the famous, but now defunct, Robinson & Cleaver's department store in the centre of Belfast. Alex was the second child, and he followed in the footsteps of his father, uncle and several cousins as he became a painter and decorator. Robert, or Bob as he was known, ventured into architecture and built one of the earliest modern style bungalows on the outskirts of Belfast where the family went to live in the 1950s. Brian ventured farther from home and joined the Royal Air Force where he quickly rose to the rank of Flight Lieutenant and a flight navigator with distinguished service.

The day to day running of the shop was interrupted when Mrs. Woods was admitted to hospital for possible surgery. On discovering she was expecting a baby the surgery was cancelled. Another patient in a neighbouring bed commented to Mrs. Woods, "The good Lord must have something special for this child." Her casual comment was to be fulfilled in a way that no one in the family could ever have imagined.

Bill was born in October 1937. As the youngest of the five children he has vivid memories of the busy, noisy and often boisterous home. Like many boys of that day playing Cowboys and Indians occupied a lot of their free time. They would hide behind settees and chairs and shoot imaginary arrows across the room in answer to the illusory sounds of gunfire. Bill as a baby was sometimes made the unwitting victim of an ambush as his pram was used by his brothers as an imaginary stagecoach.

In September of 1939, almost two years after Bill was born, Britain declared war on Germany. Like many other Ulstermen Mr. Woods volunteered to serve his country in the navy. With a shop to manage, a home to run, five small children to rear and now her husband gone off to war, the help of Aunt Eve, one of Mrs. Woods' sisters, was very much appreciated. She moved to live with the family. Eve became a favourite aunt and nanny to the children and made a big impression on young Bill. She remained a greatly loved and respected person throughout her years.

Managing a shop in the war years was made even more difficult than in the depression of the 1930s because of the introduction of ration books and limited quotas for customers. Added to this were the dark clouds of war which cast a sense of gloom and depression over the city where the nearby shipyards of Harland and Wolff, also in East Belfast, were a prime target for bombing. Many people were evacuated to rural parts of Ulster. This often meant families were divided as the children were taken to the countryside while parents remained at their employment in the city.

This presented a dilemma for Mrs. Woods. Her husband had gone off to the war front, and four of her children, Nina, Alex, Bob and Brian, were evacuated to Curryfree in the Sperrin Mountains of County Londonderry. Bill was too young to be sent away so he remained at home at the rear of the shop with Aunt Eve and his mother who continued to manage her shop. The war scattered the Woods family, and Mrs. Woods found it difficult to bear the separation from her children. The weekend visits to far off Curryfree were exciting for young Bill when he roamed the surrounding hills with his brothers. However, there were a lot of tears when the visit ended and the contingent from Belfast had to take the long bus ride back to the city.

It was this separation that prompted Mrs. Woods to sell her business and look for alternative accommodation, preferably out of the city where the children would be safe from potential bombing raids. She decided to explore the possibility of somewhere to rent in Ballygowan, a rural village nestled in the rolling hills of the beautiful County Down, eight miles south of Belfast. Several visits were made to the village, but all properties were fully occupied with no likelihood of any becoming vacant. However, it was pointed out to Mrs. Woods that there was one property available, but it was unlikely she would be interested. Many people had refused to live in the property because of local superstition of it being a haunted house. The house was named Ardcarron which is better known today as the The Old School House and is located near to the centre of the town. The large black granite stone edifice, which belonged to the Presbyterian Church, had originally been built as a school for girls. It stands four stories high and is to this day the most imposing landmark on the undulating countryside around Ballygowan.

Undaunted by the local rumour of ghosts or anything spooky, Mrs. Woods, always ready for a challenge, decided that having her children around her in the calm and quiet of Ballygowan was worth the risk. Nina, Alex, Bob and Brian were brought from the Sperrins; all furniture and personal belongings were removed from the cornershop and transported to Ballygowan. Mrs. Woods, Aunt Eve and the children were together again.

The family remained in Ballygowan for most of the war, not just as tenants in the imposing granite building, but Mrs. Woods put to good use her acquired commercial and managerial skills to run the school house for the many families who came to reside within its stout walls during the dark days of World War II. At times it ran with clock-work efficiency as well as any guest house. On other occasions the escapades of the occupants would have provided a script worthy of a "Fawlty Towers" television comedy.

The Old School House was divided into three parts. One wing was the residence of the headmaster Mr. Jacob Haire, a bachelor and well known figure in the local community. This residence was immediately adjacent to the school which occupied the main central part of the building. The other wing of the school gave ample housing for families evacuated from Belfast. The entrance to the school was at the base of a central tower, at the top of which was a large clock that had recently been donated to the town by the distinguished Senator J. Hill Dickson of a well known local family. Above the clock large white letters contrasted against the black granite to boldly spell out the appropriate Bible text, "The Time is Short."

Time did not seem short for the Woods' children who were as happy as the days were long. They thought the spacious rooms and long corridors of the large school were like paradise after the small rooms at the rear of a corner shop. There was plenty of space to run, play and even to ride bicycles up and down the corridors. On weekends uncles, aunts and cousins came to spend a few days, and when Belfast was victim of Hitler's blitz, up to nearly a hundred people, mostly relatives, joined the Woods in the old school house. Each family was allocated a classroom for their accommodation.

When the Woods and their cousins, the Robinsons, got together there was some fun and at times nearly a riot. The reputed discovery of a skeleton in a cavity of a wall in the old building led to endless stories of the haunted house. The boys made the most of the reputation and spiced up stories and fantasies into strike fear in all who came to stay with them.

Some families stayed for a short time and others for a few years. One of those who stayed longest was Miss Norah Mercer from Newry. She was a primary school teacher and had been appointed to teach at the nearby Magherscuse Primary School. Dr. McLarin, the local Presbyterian minister, visited Miss Mercer when she spent some weeks in hospital and suggested she might think of convalescing at Ardcarron when she was released. Her initial plan was to stay a few days until she would move back to her own place. Those few days of hospitality were drawn out to nearly four years, and the school mistress loved every minute of it.

At first it was strange for the boys to have a school mistress living in the same house with the family, but soon they enjoyed it. Together the teacher and children climbed the stairs every night to the first floor where they had their bedrooms. The boys then led a cavalry charge against Miss Mercer's room on their imaginary horses. It was their way of saying goodnight. Next morning Miss Mercer chased them down the corridor and had them on the run — that was her good morning to the children.

Alex and Bob studied at Downpatrick High School while young Brian and Bill attended Ballygowan Primary School. In the evenings Miss Mercer made a valiant contribution for young Bill to learn the "three R's" of reading, writing and `rithmatic although Bill maintains he was seven years old before he learned to read.

Outside the classroom and away from the extra lessons Miss Mercer was like a member of the family and entered into all its activities of both work and play. The family often gave her an embarrassed red face as they tried to match her with the bachelor neighbour, Mr. Jacob Haire the headmaster. She took it all in good fun and learned to play along with their teasing. Throughout Bill's adult years in Brazil Miss Mercer never failed to send him a birthday card. However, Bill confesses that he never remembered to return one to her. He should have remembered, for both he and Miss Mercer shared the same birthday date.

Most boys are mischievous, and the four Woods boys were no exception. Often the fights were merciless and uncompromising, and yet they were equally quick and loyal to defend each other against outsiders. Bill was always able to boast of three big brothers when he got into difficulties with other boys.

The number of different people who came to stay gave the boys a lot of expertise in playing pranks on the unsuspecting visitors. One memorable and mischievous prank was Brian's penny which had a hole bored in its centre. When the boys were sent to the local Presbyterian Church on Sunday Mrs. Woods gave each child a penny for their collection. At the appropriate time when the offering was announced Brian was well prepared. He volunteered to put a coin into the offering plate for all the boys. Ingeniously he had the pierced penny attached to an elastic string up his sleeve. When the offering plate passed along their pew he placed his penny on the plate only to have it immediately spring back up his sleeve unnoticed by the church steward. With the resulting profit all the boys bought sweets. Mrs. Woods never could figure out where the boys got money to buy sweets on Sundays.

Football is always a favourite sport for boys, and one day when they were having a kick-about at the headmaster's end of the building, a misguided kick sent the ball smashing through the window of Mr. Haire's bathroom—while Mr. Haire was still in the bath. Brian climbed up to the window and saw the not too amused headmaster sitting in a predicament. Through the broken glass Brian requested from the shocked and embarrassed headmaster, "Mr. Haire, can we have our ball back?"

On another occasion a painter was contracted to paint the clock at the highest part of the tower. In the course of his work he was slightly intimidated by the boys. Alex looked up the high ladder and casually said to the painter, "The last time a painter went up that ladder he fell to the ground, and we had to scrape his remains off the steps!"

Perhaps it was in Ballygowan that Bill had the first influences of the Gospel on his young heart. The family worshipped at Ballygowan Presbyterian Church, but the children attended Sunday School at Tullygirvan Mission Hall. One distinct memory of those days was attending special evangelistic meetings conducted in Ballygowan by two of Ulster's distinguished evangelists, Mr. Bert Wheeler and Mr. Matt Boland. For Bill the memory of that mission was greatly underscored because some of Bill's cousins and brothers made a profession of faith in Jesus Christ as a result of those meetings.

Another fact that etched the memory of the mission on Bill's young mind was that Mr. Boland shared the same birth date as Bill and Miss Mercer, and Mr. Boland made a lot of banter and jest of this coincidence.

A local lad whose family shared the facilities of the Old School House was young Harry Reid. Bill attended school with Harry's brother Tom. Neither Bill nor Harry could ever have dreamed that from the quiet County Down village they would both go on to be missionaries in Brazil's Amazon jungles—Harry with the Brethren Assemblies and Bill with missionaries who in those early days were already in the process of founding the Acre Gospel Mission.

While the family was seeing out the war in the relative safety of the quiet country town of Ballygowan, Mr. Woods was away from home at the war front. For his gallantry as a gunner on board the Empire Hope and courage in fighting a fire aboard the ship he was awarded the DSM (Distinguished Service Medal) by His Majesty King George VI and was twice mentioned in the Oak Leaf.

With the invasion of Europe by the Allied Forces in 1944 the threat of air raids and blitzing in Belfast ceased. To Mrs. Woods it seemed be an opportune time to return to the city and venture once more into the retail business. Aunt Eve married and went to live in England while Mrs. Woods secured a grocery shop on the familiar Ravenhill Road.   Bill was transferred from the Ballygowan Primary School to Nettlefield Primary School which was nearby his new Belfast home.

As they had done before the war, so again the family lived at the rear of the shop which they found to be rather confined after being used to the spacious building at Ballygowan. Because of the lack of space the family remained living at the rear of the shop for only a short while and then moved to several different residences in East Belfast until they finally settled in Houston Drive on the Castlereagh Road. This move was to greatly influence the unfolding of Bill's spiritual future.

Chapter Three

All Things New

❖

Following the end of World War II there was phenomenal growth in the Belfast Battalion of the Boys Brigade (BB) and in the corresponding Girl's Brigade. These uniformed organisations offered young people a variety of physical activities such as gymnastics, soccer and marching drills, plus Sunday parades when the boys and girls marched to Church. Besides these physical activities the avowed primary aim of the movement was, and is, the "advancement of Christ's Kingdom amongst young men."

The 30th Company of the Boys Brigade associated with Orangefield Presbyterian Church was near to Bill's new home at Houston Drive. Bill not only attended the church but became a recruit of the 30th BB Company which endeavoured to fulfil the Brigade's primary objective. Under the leadership of the Company's Captain, Mr. Fred McCormick who was known to all at Orangefield as Pop McCormick, many boys were won for the Saviour and quite a few of these went into Christian work.

Evangelical conversion is generally regarded as a sudden, radical and spiritual experience like that of Saul of Tarsus on the

Road to Damascus. However, it is also true that often there are many links in the chain of events that lead to a genuine conversion. Even Saul of Tarsus, who consented to and oversaw the execution of Stephen, was greatly affected by the manner in which the first Christian martyr accepted his cruel death. Stephen's dying prayer was a link in the chain of events that led to the conversion of the great apostle.

Jim Hanna, Bill's Sunday School teacher at Orangefield Presbyterian Church, was another one of the vital links in the chain that would eventually lead to Bill's conversion along with Pop McCormick. Beside the weekly Bible Class on Sunday mornings and the devotional talk on the activity night, the Sunday School Teacher and the Captain enthusiastically employed every opportunity to bring the boys to Jesus Christ.

In 1948 the famous Canadian evangelist, Dr. Oswald J. Smith, conducted an evangelistic crusade in the neighbouring McQuiston Memorial Presbyterian Church. The large church was packed to capacity night after night, and Dr. Smith preached with dynamic power on the great themes of the Christian Gospel. Captain Fred McCormick spared no effort to bring his boys under the influence of Dr. Smith's preaching.

Although Bill was still a young boy, his tender heart was greatly touched in those meetings, and one night after the evangelist preached from John 3:16 about the love of God, Bill went forward to the enquiry room. A counsellor read with him and gave him an appropriate booklet. Even though some of Bill's friends were saved in those meetings and Bill spoke to a counsellor he did not experience conversion at that time.

An interesting fact about those meetings is that just about that time in 1948 Dr. Smith received an invitation from Mr. Rodheaver, the famed American hymn writer and evangelist, to compose verses around the words "Then Jesus came." Dr. Smith at first hesitated, but within a few days he presented a hymn that was to be sung around the world by leading Christian vocalists.

The first lines of that hymn expressed the experience of Blind Bartimaeus to whom Jesus miraculously restored sight. Bill Woods could not have known in those meetings that one day he would be involved in restoring sight to many, who like Bartimaeus, had suffered blindness for most of their lives. Another lesson Bill remembers from those bygone days is that Pop McCormick said how ironic it was that the Egyptians should have paid Moses' mother, Jochebed, to do what she wanted to do — raise her own son. Bill remembered that story years later when he realised that he being was paid by the Brazilian Government to do what he had always wanted to do — bring relief to those who suffer blindness like Bartimaeus did.

One of the important dates of the BB calendar was the annual Camp in July when boys slept under canvas for one or two weeks in a prearranged location. Bill remembers that another important link in the chain leading to his conversion was the camp at Kirkcaldy in Scotland. Although it was a week of fun and games, and drills and marches, there was a lot of spiritual input as each day began with a devotional at which the Gospel was clearly presented. Likewise in the evenings there was a similar measure of evangelistic emphasis. Bill was in a turmoil. He was so conscious of his need of a Saviour and yet was too afraid to take the all important step.

Prior to the Kirkcaldy Camp Bill's family moved back to reside on the Ravenhill Road. Anne Robinson, his cousin, invited Bill and his brother Bob to attend the Sunday evening services at Ravenhill Free Presbyterian Church. The two brothers accepted the invitation and at the meeting were absolutely captivated and amused by the eccentricity of the preacher, the Rev. Ian R. K. Paisley. So taken were they with the preaching they decided to return again.

The young Ian Paisley was unorthodox in his style of preaching and powerful in his delivery. He strode up and down the long platform at the front of the church, and on occasions, while yet preaching, he came down out of the pulpit and pleaded with those who occupied the front pews to come to Jesus Christ—such was the preacher's passion and fervour for men and women to come to Jesus Christ for salvation. Mr. Paisley's preaching was decisive and dynamic, and he made Bible truths come to life. His sermon titles were also unorthodox, at times amusing and often aroused a lot of public interest. Bill remembers some of those sermons:

"Giving the Pigs a Permanent Wave." (The parable of the Prodigal Son waving good-bye to the pigs when he returned to his father. Luke 15)

"One Man in Hell and Five on the Road!" (The account of the rich man who from hell prayed for his five brothers. Luke 16)

"Demons in Pigskin Swim Suits." (The report of how demons expelled from the demoniac of Gadarra entered into the swine and rushed into the sea. Mark 5)

"Two Fools and a Hen-pecked Husband." (The parable of the great supper and the invited guests who made groundless excuses not to attend. Luke 14)

"How the Devil's Postman got Saved." (Paul's conversion as he took letter's of authority to persecute Christians in Damascus. (Acts 9)

Many people were converted in these services.

Bill continued to attend and soon his amusement gave way to spiritual concern and a deep conviction that he needed to accept Jesus Christ as his personal Saviour. Through Mr. Paisley's preaching Bill learned that Jesus Christ

became poor that we might become rich;
(James 2:5)

was born at Bethlehem that we might be born again;
(John 1:14)

became a Servant that we might become sons of God;
(Galatians 4:6,7)

had no earthly home that we might have a heavenly home;
(Matthew 8:20)

was made sin that we might be made righteous;
(2 Corinthians 5:21)

died on a cruel cross that we might live an abundant life.
(John 5:24,25)

On the Sunday following the Kirkcaldy Camp Bill attended the evening evangelistic service at the Ravenhill Church as he had been doing for almost three months. After Mr. Paisley preached he made a public invitation for those who were willing to come to Christ. As the congregation sang the invitation hymn a conflict raged in Bill's heart and mind, I want to accept the Saviour. I am afraid of what people will think. How will they take it at home? What will Brian say? Does Jesus really love me so much? The invitation hymn continued as did Mr. Paisley's appeal while these thoughts rushed through Bill's mind and weighed on his heart.

Finally there was a rush of desire and courage to do what was right, and in response to the appeal Bill went forward to the small enquiry room. There Mr. Jim Weatherall led him to personal faith in Jesus Christ. That unforgettable date was the 20th July, 1952.

For some weeks only people at the church knew of Bill's conversion. To all at home Bill had always appeared to be a good boy but they soon perceived there was a change in his behaviour—he wanted to be with Christian friends; church took the place of the cinema, and his newly acquired habit of reading the Bible seemed strange. All the family wanted to know what made the difference in his life. When he finally told them the reason, it was not welcomed at first. No one in the family felt Bill needed to be converted. He had always been sent to church. Nevertheless, Bill persevered to live out his new found life in Jesus Christ.

At this time Bill was a pupil at Belfast High School and when he told his friends he had become a Christian he lost some former companions. This loss was neutralised by the fact he soon found some new Christian friends in Victor Glenn and Audrey Newell who also attended the same school. They encouraged each other in their Christian lives in what seemed to be an arena of sceptics and infidels.

Coming to Jesus Christ was only the first step of many taken by faith. For Bill the Christian life continued to be a daily walk of faith with Jesus Christ leading him to maturity in the Saviour. He also found that although he was a Christian there was a constant struggle in his heart. Being a Christian does not make a person perfect in this world, and Bill was only too conscious of his own failures. Two opposing forces seemed to be locked in continual conflict in his life. The flesh, representing the old life, assailed him with doubts, fears and temptations. On the other hand he wanted to walk with the Lord, serve the Lord and please Him.

By reading the Scriptures he learned early that he could overcome the world, the flesh and the devil only as he yielded to the

Saviour. In all this Bill endeavoured to be practical and realistic. He wanted to live separate from the world and yet not lose touch with those in the world. He wanted to live above sin and yet within the reach of sinners around him. He also soon discovered the importance of maintaining a close relationship with his Lord in having a daily quiet time. This discipline did not come easily, but after forty-five years as a Christian it is still a daily habit Bill seeks to maintain.

Out of school Bill encountered most encouragement with his Christian friends in the Young People's Fellowship at the Ravenhill Free Presbyterian Church. Unknown to him the influence of these meetings and the young people at the church were crucial in shaping his future plans.

Chapter Four

Getting Involved

❖

B eing the youngest of four bright, intelligent and fun-loving brothers gave Bill a distinct disadvantage at Belfast High School. The foregoing pranks and wrong doings of his brothers made Bill appear to be an obvious threat to the school discipline. When another "Woods" appeared on the roll book on Bill's first day at Belfast High School, he was called to sit in the front desk where the teacher could keep a careful eye on him. The teacher was not risking any chances on this Woods boy after brother Brian had been in the class the previous year. On the other hand, Brian and Bob's high scoring performance in most school exams set high standards for Bill as he followed one year behind Brian right through his school years.

Studies were also accompanied by hard work after school hours. Mrs. Woods had taken the responsibility to clean a doctor's surgery, and Bill was made a reluctant conscript to help. With much perseverance and study in an attempt to emulate Bob and Brian in his school work, Bill completed his course at Belfast High School. He eventually gained Junior and Senior Certificates of Higher Education, which at the time gave him opportunity to follow on to University.

Already Bill as a Christian had felt a stirring desire to be a foreign missionary so he preferred to think of going to Bible College instead of university or college. Mr. and Mrs. Woods believed Bible College was not in Bill's best interests and tried to persuade him to go to Stranmillis Teacher Training College in Belfast, but he was resolute in his decision to go to Bible College and be a missionary rather than study to be a teacher.

Having resolved not to proceed with teacher training or a university education and having not been allowed to go for missionary training, Bill applied for nursing at Belfast's City Hospital believing this would be of great benefit to him one day when he would eventually reach the Mission Field. However, Mrs. Woods was equally determined that if Bill was not going to pursue teacher training he most certainly was not going to do nursing so that door was rigidly blocked.

During the ensuing debate about Bill's future career he secured a job at Harry Ferguson's Tyres in Belfast's city centre and soon was immersed in the work of invoicing and dispatching tyres to all parts of Northern Ireland. He was glad to find that in the office there was a fine Christian lady who not only set a good example but was also a big encouragement to him. Miss Jean Greer not only befriended Bill during the short time at Harry Ferguson's Tyres, but later, and until the time she died of Multiple Sclerosis, Jean and her family became firm supporters of Bill's work abroad.

Although he was set up in what seemed to be a comfortable job and had some money in his pocket each week, selling tyres for the rest of his life was not what God had planned for Bill nor was it what he wanted. At the Ravenhill Church he not only became a member of the Young People's Fellowship, but he also got very involved in all the activities of the Church. Besides the fellowship meetings there were early morning and late night prayer meetings. There also were Bible Study evenings and always special evangelistic efforts. Bill missed none of these. Outreach from the church also engaged Bill in evangelism by tract distribution to the local community and on Saturday and Sunday evenings he attended an open air meeting at the gates of the nearby Ormeau Park.

It was at one of these open air meetings that Bill had his initiation into public speaking. The church group stood in a semi-circle around a microphone which was duly set in the centre. From the microphone the leader of the meeting conducted the proceedings. Often he would have a pre-arranged programme for the meeting, but frequently there was an impromptu call to the microphone for one of the Christians present to either sing or give testimony of their conversion to Jesus Christ. It always seemed that the more mature saints were accorded this opportunity. Bill had never spoken in public before and felt relatively anonymous hiding in the crowd. Being a shy young lad he felt his role was solely to make up the number in the semi-circle.

One night after singing another rousing hymn the leader of the meeting made an unexpected announcement over the loudspeaker, "Our brother Bill Woods will come now and give his testimony."

At that moment Bill seemed to freeze to the ground, and when he realised it was his name that had been called and everyone was waiting for him to step forward, his first reaction was, "How do I get out of here?"

With a push in the back from a well intentioned brother in the group, Bill was thrust in to the middle of the circle and trembling before the lone microphone, he stammered out a few words, "The twentieth of July, nineteen fifty-two." (This was the date of his conversion.) He could say no more, so with his head down he shyly beat a hasty retreat to the shelter and security of the semi-circle and hid his face in the crowd.

That first unexpected and what seemed disastrous taste of public speaking encouraged Bill to venture into more active service for his Saviour. With his cousin Anne Robinson, Edna Marshall and Willie Townley, he formed the Victory Testimony Band. Belfast at that time was ripe soil for budding preachers and testimony groups who were always available to sing, testify and lead meetings. Bill received much of his early experience as a preacher in these meetings. Many smaller churches and Mission Halls were glad to welcome them to conduct their Sunday services or the midweek fellowship hour.

One such meeting place was in a barn at Magherscuse near to Ballygowan where Bill had spent part of his childhood. The leaders of the Mission Hall were daring enough to invite the Victory Testimony Band to conduct an evangelistic mission at the barn. It was a daunting challenge for the recently formed group of inexperienced preachers, but they felt God would have them accept the invitation. The two week mission was well attended, and on the Sunday evenings numbers were so good people had to stand outside the Hall. God answered prayer during this special evangelistic effort and many people were won for Jesus Christ as a result of the meetings.

One lasting result of that mission was the conversion to Christ of Mr. Jim Douglas. Jim was a local lad who attended the meetings with his sister Jean. Like Jim, Jean also trusted the Saviour as a consequence of the meetings. Both Jim and Jean were keen for the Lord and took an interest in another local fellow and eventually were instrumental in leading him to personal faith in Jesus Christ. Jean's interest in this new convert grew until she eventually married him. That new convert was Mr. Jim Garret who currently is the pastor at Portrush Baptist Church in Northern Ireland. Jim and Jean's son Stephen is pastor at Sion Mills Baptist Church. Jim Douglas and his family worship at Comber Baptist Church where Jim has served as a deacon for many years, and he still maintains an active interest in Bill's work abroad.

The Rev. Paisley was very involved in evangelistic campaigns across Ulster in the 1950s, and Bill was one of a ready band of workers who helped in those revival meetings. Sometimes they accompanied Ian Paisley on the bus or on bicycles to Dunmurry or Whiteabbey, and on a few occasions Bill was invited to substitute for the evangelist when Mr. Paisley was not able to be present. This indicated the further development of Bill's preaching capacity.

During another evangelistic mission at Ballygowan Mr. Paisley could not complete the second week of the mission, and he asked Bill to preach for him that week. In all of these missions scores of people were won for Jesus Christ. Free Presbyterian churches were established in Dunmurry and Whiteabbey as a result of these endeavours.

The mission at Ballygowan concluded with an outstanding weekend conference at which Fred Orr, recently home from Brazil, and Emma Munn, a veteran missionary from West Africa, took part with Mr. Paisley and Bill. As a result of that conference a weekly prayer meeting was established that eventually led to the founding of the Ballygowan Free Presbyterian Church.

The new Free Presbyterian congregation in Whiteabbey which today is known as Newtownabbey Free Presbyterian Church, occupied the town's former court house for their weekly meetings. Mr. Paisley asked Bill to help the new part time pastor, Mr. Cecil Harvey from Crossgar, by playing the organ at the weekly services. This was a commitment that Bill willingly took on in spite of being nervous about his abilities as an organist. The source of heat in the former court house was a large fire at the front of the main hall where the meetings were conducted. While Bill played it seemed at times the burning coals whistled to the tune of the rousing hymns.

Cecil and Bill travelled together to and from Whiteabbey every Sunday for two years; Cecil also had his tea at Bill's home every Friday night, and from there they drove to the church for the weekly prayer meeting. This close working association with the Harvey's forged a lasting friendship with Cecil and his wife May who later were responsible for Bill's prayer letter when he left for Brazil.

To help him with his weekly undertaking at the organ Bill attended music lessons with Miss Mollie Miskimmin of Cicero Gardens, Belfast. Bill, with typical wit and modestly, tells that one day she complained to him about not being able to open her windows. Bill volunteered to look at them for her and found that the sash cords were rotted. He gallantly changed all the cords for her, and soon the windows were opening and closing smoothly. The following day Bill was back for a music lesson, and in the course of her instruction Miss Miskimmin suggested, "Bill, I think you might be better sticking to working with windows rather than following a career in music."

In truth, Miss Miskimmin, marvelled at Bill's ability to play better when he closed the music book than when the book was open. As a teacher and friend she was a great help to him. She cried when Bill finally announced he had to terminate his music lessons because he was leaving for Bible School. She was so disappointed she was losing his weekly visits.

Chapter Five

Eyes Opened to the Mission Field

❖

Belfast in the 1950s was a hub of evangelistic fervour, Bible preaching, expository teaching, prophetic conferences and missionary challenge. The Jack Shuler Crusade at Belfast's largest auditorium, the Kings Hall, was the biggest evangelistic gathering that Ulster had ever known when in June 1955 the American evangelist conducted the Crusade in glorious summer weather. Hundreds of people were converted and the impact of the Crusade was felt for the following decade.

Well known preachers visited Northern Ireland from Scotland, England and the United States; there also were able Bible teachers in Ulster such W. E. Tocher, Pastor Willie Mullen and Pastor Hugh Orr who drew large congregations to their packed churches for weekly Bible studies and conducted Bible teaching conferences across the Province. All night prayer meetings were a feature of evangelical church life and open-air meetings were conducted in the public parks and at street corners. Missionary valedictory and welcome home services were held frequently as Ulster was a prime sending and supporting base for foreign missions.

All these aspects of the spiritual awakening in that decade were also abundantly evident in the Ravenhill Road Free Presbyterian Church where large crowds flocked to hear Ian Paisley preach. Bill was only one of many zealous young workers at the church. Bertie Cook, John Douglas, Campbell Smith, Tom McClelland, Lily Warick, Meta Telford, Ross Harbinson, Valerie Shaw, Tom and Betty Cross and Maurice Caughey are but some who were members of the Ravenhill Young People's Fellowship at that time who subsequently went into full-time Christian work, several to the home ministry and the others to various mission fields around the world.

Bill was repeatedly challenged by the dedication of missionaries who visited the church. The first missionary he heard was Miss Mollie Harvey who had recently returned from Brazil. Mollie had been a co-founder of the Acre Gospel Mission with Mr. and Mrs. William McComb and her devotional messages about her work in the Amazon were to be an early forerunner of the path that Bill would ultimately follow to be one of her colleagues in Brazil.

Mr. Willie Weir, formerly a missionary in India and the Northern Ireland representative of the World-wide Evangelization Crusade (WEC), was also a frequent speaker at the various meetings at Ravenhill. Mr. Weir's appeal for a life of full surrender to Jesus Christ did not fall on deaf ears. His missionary challenge at the Ravenhill church resulted in Bill being a regular prayer partner at the Tuesday night WEC prayer battery at Glandore Avenue in north Belfast. From the Ravenhill Church several missionaries were already serving with the WEC; David and Maude Carson and Ross Harbinson served in Liberia; Jim and Maureen Murray were in East Africa

The Munn family had perhaps the greatest impact on Bill's youth. Emma and Janet Munn had served God with great distinction in West Africa and their lives, which were sold out to God and the missionary cause, inspired Bill as he listened to them tell of God's provision, guidance and protection during their years on the African mission fields. Robert Munn later invited Bill to join him for summer work at the Lammerle Bible School in France where he and his wife also served the Lord.

Emma Munn's zeal and enthusiasm were not only to be a life long inspiration to Bill but they were greatly reflected in the life of her younger sister and brother-in-law, who were equally dedicated to the Lord. Ernie and Jessie Eades served God in the Cape Verde Islands with the Church of the Nazarene along with yet another Munn sister, Mrs. Lottie Gaye.

At one of the frequent Missionary Rallies in the church Mr. and Mrs. Eades were invited to conduct the meeting. On that night Jessie gave her testimony of how her mother had prayed for all the family that God would not only save but use them. God had answered a mother's prayers in a super abundant manner as blessings were mixed with tragedy. One son was killed during the war and another drowned the day the war ended. Five of her children, four girls and one boy, plus her own sister, went to different foreign mission fields, the remaining sisters were active as supporting prayer partners in the work. The Munns inspired and motivated a generation of Christians in Ulster to dedicate their lives to Jesus Christ and serve Him on the mission field.

On that night Jessie spoke from Nehemiah 8:10, "Go your way, eat the fat, drink the sweet, and send portions unto them for whom nothing is prepared." In the course of her report she challenged all present, "Is there a young man here who would be prepared to surrender his life to Jesus Christ and go to serve Him on some mission field?" Bill was overwhelmed by what he heard and for the first time he was sure God had called him to consecrate his life to full-time missionary service.

Another circumstance was to mark a milestone in confirming Bill's call to the mission field; at the nearby Mount Merrion Free Presbyterian Church the Rev. David Brown had invited Fred and Ina Orr to conduct an evangelistic mission. Fred and Ina had recently returned from two years missionary training at the WEC Missionary Training College in Glasgow and were accepted candidates for the work of the Acre Gospel Mission in Brazil. Bill at that time was a Sunday School teacher at the Mount Merrion Church and attended many of the meetings during Fred and Ina's Mission.

Those meetings were greatly blessed by the Lord as Fred preached every night and Ina, gifted with a beautiful voice, sang some of the great Gospel hymns. As a result of God's blessing on the meetings many felt the meetings should be extended for several more weeks.

One of the highlights of the mission was the night which was dedicated to messages in song by Ina. The most requested hymn that night was the "The Love of God" in which Ina gave tremendous expression to the profound depths of God's immeasurable love. Another hymn that Ina sang that night and would sing again the night before she and Fred left for Brazil in March 1954 was "Let me Burn Out for Thee Dear Lord."

O Lord the world is lost in sin and few there be who care
Many of whom profess Thy Name no burden will help to bare.
We need passion Lord for souls to bring the lost back to Thee
Our hearts must be stirred 'til all have heard, at least once of Calvary.

Let me burn out for Thee dear Lord burn and wear out for Thee
Don't let me rust or my life be a failure my God to Thee
Use me and all I have dear Lord And get me so close to Thee
'Til I feel the throb of the great heart of God and my life burns out for Thee.

That last hymn and prayer of Ina's before leaving for South America was answered in sad and ironic circumstances. As she and Fred journeyed up the Amazon River and its tributaries Ina became very ill and as they approached the town of Labrea a high fever caused her to pass into the presence of her Lord. She was only twenty-nine years old.

News of Ina's premature home call on 4 June 1954, so soon after her arrival in Brazil, shocked the evangelical community in Northern Ireland and beyond. People's sympathy, thoughts and prayers were with Fred who remained in Brazil and with her family at home. Ina's mother, Mrs. McMurry, would never see her darling daughter on earth again. At the Mount Merrion and Ravenhill Churches there was not only stunned shock, but also a deep challenge for other young people to follow the example set by Ina Orr and give their lives to "burn out for Jesus Christ."

Bill Woods was not found wanting when God called him in the wake of this tragic news. However, this was no easy step. Besides the anguish of leaving his family and friends at the church, it also meant the dissolving of a four year relationship with a young Christian lady who felt her health would not permit her to live in the tropics. The pain of parting was not easy.

Chapter Six

Missionary Training

---------------- ❖ ----------------

A bove the entrance to 10 Prince Albert Road, Glasgow, in
bold and large white letters was the Bible text "Have Faith
In God." (Mark 11:22) The day in January, 1957 when
Bill passed below that text to make his entrance into the large four
story grey house that stood on the grounds was a big step of faith for
a novice. In days to come he would have to translate that Bible
quotation from the bold painted letters above the entrance into his
personal and daily experience.

This house was the home of the World-wide Evangelization Crusade (WEC) Missionary Training College (MTC) which had been
founded by Mr. and Mrs. Francis Rowbotham. Fran and Ma Row,
as the Rowbothams were known, had been a living demonstration
of practical and daring faith in God. Owners of a grocery business
in Sparkbrook, Birmingham, they had been challenged by Rees
Howells at a WEC Conference at the Bible College of Wales in
Swansea to forsake all and follow the Saviour. They did exactly
that and in 1937 went to Columbia with the WEC.

After two years of service in South America they were invited to be representatives for the mission in United States. With the outbreak of war it was not possible to go to the USA and subsequently in 1942 Fran and Ma Row were invited by Mr. Norman Grubb to pioneer the Scottish representation of their mission.

They went to live in Glasgow and after diligent deputation and much prayer they had organised a thriving prayer meeting, or prayer battery as it was called, with many young people in attendance. As the Lord raised up missionary candidates for the various WEC fields, Fran and Ma Row felt they should open a training school to prepare others for the expanding work of the Crusade. Firmly trusting in God's faithfulness they proved God's miraculous provision in the acquiring of the premises at 10 Prince Albert Road, in Hynland, one of the best residential areas of Glasgow. The house had been formerly owned by the Blackie family, well known in Scotland and owners of one of the foremost publishing companies in Great Britain. At this address the family had given hospitality to Dwight L. Moody and Ira Sankey during their evangelistic campaigns in Scotland.

Bill's decisions to leave employment and go to the college were difficult to make. In the Scriptures divine guidance is equated as an inward testimony of the Holy Spirit that we are the children of God. "For as many are led by the Spirit of God, they are the sons of God." (Rom. 8:14) Time and again God confirmed to Bill that was the way he was to follow. At first when he announced at home he was hoping to go to the mission field his father jokingly ridiculed, "The mission field? You'll be lucky if you get to the potato fields."

Notwithstanding the discouragement and having felt the constraint of God's call on his life, Bill diligently enquired about the various possibilities of Bible college training. After he had gleaned some information from various friends he concluded that the WEC MTC was the place God would have him attend. He applied and was accepted to start in September, 1956. This step of faith proved to be the first of many which had to be crossed.

The first hurdle was one he met at home where his parents were still of the opinion Bill would be better off going to University.

Because of the government's new policy recently introduced at that time, no money would need to be paid for course books which were required for university, whereas to go to a fee paying Bible college without any guaranteed finance seemed a ludicrous decision to Mr. and Mrs. Woods.   Mr. Paisley paid a visit to the home and assured Bill's parents that all would be well with their son.   Bill reluctantly agreed to wait until after his ninteenth birthday before leaving for Scotland for Bible School.

Bill seemed to be a forlorn figure that January night when as a boy of nineteen he boarded the ship for Glasgow. He did not feel he was alone for he was sure he was stepping out in obedience to God and was assured of the promise of God's presence with him. The Lord always seems to have His servants in every place and on the overnight boat journey to Glasgow Bill was accompanied by the American evangelist John Wesley White who later would become an evangelist with the Billy Graham Evangelistic Association. Dr. White, who married a Belfast girl and was very active in evangelistic campaigns and rallies both in Ulster and Scotland, was God's instrument to encourage the young Bill Woods who was stepping out on the threshold of his career.

The college had been in operation for ten years when Bill arrived in January 1957. Already many graduates of MTC such as Brother Andrew of God's Smuggler fame, and others were making a great impact in many countries around the world. Mr. Stewart Dinnen was the principal of the college and was ably assisted by residential staff and visiting lecturers. Bible study and homiletic classes were given a priority in the daily lectures. Practical work on motor mechanics, plumbing, carpentry, building etc. were all included in the curriculum plus classes in tropical hygiene and phonetics. Although not always appreciated at the time, all these subjects proved to be of great value in years to come.

However, the greatest lessons of those two years in college were the lessons of faith, of fellowship, of prayer and of sacrifice which were both exemplified and encouraged by Fran and Ma Rowbotham. Besides trusting God to meet his daily needs and the quarterly payment of his fees, Bill with the other students learned to trust God for the supply of building materials for an extension to the college. At times their faith seemed weak as the students met to pray for the materials to complete the new wing of the building which would serve as a dormitory for the boys on the ground floor and a dining room above. God, who owns the cattle on all the hills and the gold of every mine, had His ways and His servants in every place. The needs were always met and quite often at the very last minute. These experiences would be repeated in Bill's personal life and ministry many times in the future.

The morning devotional talks from Stuart Dinnen and visiting WEC leaders and missionaries returning from the various fields emphasised the importance of the Christian's crucified life with Christ. This meant dying to self, denying one's own plans and taking up the cross and following the Master. It was the essence of sacrificial living as patterned in Christ, who came not to be ministered unto but to minister and give His life a ransom for many. This self denial was evident in the staff and was encouraged in the students. The foregoing of personal plans and realising of dreams were later to be a painful part of Bill Woods' life.

The student body at MTC was made up of those who came from many countries in Europe as well as from all parts of the United Kingdom. The adjustment to different accents and cultures was also a learning process. Some of the students were very serious minded while others balanced the pressure of study with some practical fun. Not surprisingly, Bill belonged to the latter group. Emma Munn whom Bill revered had always said, "A good missionary should have a good sense of humour and a bad sense of smell." I am not sure how sensitive Bill's nose is, but wit and humour which he richly inherited from his mother, have always been a positive feature of Bill's life. On occasions they got him into trouble.

One day when Bill was in the bathroom in the boys quarter of the building he heard someone in an adjacent toilet. There was an air vent in the wall between the toilet and bathroom which emerged immediately above the toilet's cistern. To throw water through the vent and drench the unsuspecting student in the adjoining toilet was an inviting temptation which Bill could not resist. He sent a pail of water splashing through the vent and waited for the angry reaction of one of the boys. The only response was an unusual and inexplicable silence. Thinking he had missed the intended victim Bill threw another bucket of water through the vent and ran. Later Bill had to admit his culpability when Neil Rowe, one of the staff members responsible for practical work and the maintenance of the building, wanted to know how a sudden surge of water came through an air vent! What made matters worse was that Neil had just got dressed for an urgent appointment and decided to conveniently use the boys bathroom instead of returning upstairs to his apartment. Having felt the first water drench the back of his neck Neil turned round to inspect the offending vent just in time to catch Bill's second attempt right between his eyes and down over his clean white shirt.

A feature of the missionary training at MTC was the annual student missions in April or May when teams of four or six were sent out to various parts of Scotland and beyond to conduct a two week evangelistic campaign. They were encouraged to live by faith for those few weeks. The team leader was given a sealed envelope with five pounds in it just in case of emergency or their faith should fail. Bill's first mission was in Gardiner Street Church of Scotland which had a Gaelic speaking congregation in the area known as Partick. The Rev. Gilles from the Isle of Lewis, a godly and gracious man, was the minister; his assistant was Mr. Raymond McKeown. These meetings were a great encouragement to the Church. Local people were converted and lasting friendships were forged.

Part of the mission experience was that the team lived together for the duration of the mission on the church premises. While the boys slept in one of the church halls they found that the rails around the choir enclosure of the main sanctuary were ideal for hanging their washing. One Sunday morning while the boys were still asleep the caretaker opened up the Church but failed to check that all was in order in the main sanctuary. The lads got a rude awakening when the Rev. Gilles knocked their door and told them it was almost time for the morning service. You can imagine the scramble to retrieve the washing in case the worshippers should think there was to be a special rag service.

Bill's second mission was at the Baptist Church in Hopeman, a small town on Scotland's Ayrshire coast. For two weeks the team worked zealously in the community. It was a difficult time with not much response. Both missions were learning experiences for Bill and the teams. There are times in Christian service when it seems the tide waters of blessing are in near to the shore. There is liberty in preaching, people are converted and the church is stirred, enthused and revived. At other times the tide seems to be far out from the shore. The preaching is hard and it seems like you are trying to drive a chariot over wet sands only to discover the wheels are off the chariot.

As the two year training course at MTC drew to a close Bill was facing the question as to where God was leading him. Quarterly WEC conferences were held at the College and every week visiting missionaries from all over the world came to challenge the students and the Christian public of the needs on their fields. Through such meetings other students seemed to have found their guidance and were already committed to different countries; Roy Spragget was on his way to Vietnam; Geoff Williams was accepted for India; Dick Steele was due to join the Red Sea Mission Team; Stuart McFadden was planning on going to the Ivory Coast; John Lawson was invited to remain in Glasgow and to join the College staff as a lecturer. What did the Lord have for Bill Woods?

To the leadership at the college it seemed unlikely that the young Belfast lad would ever make it to any foreign mission field. They even had doubts about his suitability in any Christian work at home. Twice during the process of the two year course the staff called Bill in for a personal interview and suggested to him that it would be better to return home to Belfast. They had concluded his IQ was low, he was constantly sick and was too immature for missionary work. Bill felt there was no way he could go back to his family, his friends and his church in Belfast and tell them he was dropping out. He had testified that God had called him and there was no turning back now. In spite of the considered opinions of the staff and against their judgement Bill doggedly hung in to finish the course.

Through the tragic news of the early death of Ina Orr the Lord had already challenged Bill about Brazil and the work of the Acre

Gospel Mission in the Amazon. Fred Orr, just returned from his first term of service in Brazil, came to visit the WEC MTC where he and Ina had trained seven years previously. Fred's challenging report and preaching touched many of the students and staff. Some felt God was calling them to Brazil and several did go to Brazil with WEC when they completed their training.

Not taking guidance lightly Bill wanted to be sure this was God's way for him. Being in the WEC college and listening constantly for two years to visiting WEC missionaries, Bill felt it was only fair to enquire if the WEC had plans for pioneer work in the Amazon region of South America. He talked about the matter with Len Moules, then the British Director of WEC. Len offered to write to Wesley Driver, a veteran WEC missionary in Columbia, enquiring about the possibility of room for the sort of pioneer work Bill had in mind. Bill did not know Wesley Driver nor did the missionary know Bill.

Some weeks later Len had a resigned look on his face when he showed Bill the letter he had just received in return from Wesley Driver. In the letter Wesley said to Len that taking all things into consideration the candidate should enquire about the work of the Acre Gospel Mission who were doing that sort of pioneer work on the Brazilian side of the Amazon. That was an unmistakable confirmation of the direction Bill Woods should take. Added to this the Lord gave Bill a promise, "Behold I have set before you an open door which no man can shut." That promise was soon tried and proved to be faithful.

Chapter Seven

There's Many a Slip

❖

A former generation of missionaries changed the old adage, "There's many a slip between the cup and the lip," to "There's many slip between the call and the ship." Bill was to discover how true and painful this was.

Discipline at the WEC MTC was strict with separate study areas for the girls and boys. This was balanced somewhat by a common dining room where staff and students of both sexes mingled at meal times. Although interaction between male and female students was encouraged at meal tables, romantic attachments were very much frowned on. If men and women students formed a friendship they had to "confess" it immediately to the staff and one of the two had to leave the college until the other had finished their training.

The strict rules were sometimes violated. One notable case was that of a couple who came from opposite ends of England. They studied in separate parts of one large study room where a floor to ceiling removable partition divided the male students from the female students. No distraction was permitted. However, love always finds a way. In the dark evenings the couple could see each other from opposite extremes of the brightly lit study through the reflection in the middle windows. A wave of the hand from the fellow led to a nod of the head from the girl. Soon there was a wink of the eye in the library, an exchange of friendly talk at the meal table, and love was born.

Not sure of each others feelings and not wanting to be seen talking to each other, they decided to correspond clandestinely. He wrote a letter to her and took the letter to the library. He deposited the letter in a volume of Calvin's Institutes and then at the meal table suggested to her she have a look at Calvin's works. She liked what she read and so replied and hinted to him that he should have a look at Hodge's Systematic Theology. In due time a full admission was made to the staff and the fellow had to leave until his girl friend finished the course. Eventually they married and today are serving the Lord in another part of the world.

There was no better place to find a girl who was going to the mission field than at Bible College where there were many young people who shared common goals. Bill was one of the students who met and fell in love with a lovely Christian girl who was a student in his year at the college. She too felt the call of God to Brazil. Both had fallen in love with each other but decided to be disciplined and keep the relationship low key during the remaining months of training. However, the long summer holiday gave them opportunity to get acquainted when they met at the WEC Young Warrior Camps in Northern Ireland.

College finished for Bill and his girlfriend in December 1958 and afterwards their romance blossomed. Everything seemed idyllic. Together they did meetings where Bill preached and she sang and on other occasions they testified at missionary rallies organised by the Acre Gospel Mission. The young couple seemed most suited to all who met them and they appeared to be a perfect match.

Together they made application to the Acre Gospel Mission. Both were called for their interview with the mission committee at the Kensington Hotel in Belfast. As was the custom in those days, the candidates were invited for high tea with committee members. Slightly on edge and rather apprehensive about the occasion Bill could not enjoy his tea. He was all the more uncomfortable when his foot got stuck on a piece of bread and butter which someone had dropped under the table and had conveniently ignored. Bill imagined the impression he would make on the committee if he was asked to go to the front to address them with a slice of buttered bread still stuck to his shoe. In the event he was spared that embarrassment.

After the interview of each candidate separately, the committee announced that both were accepted by the mission for the work in Brazil. There was however, a stipulation; Bill's young lady would proceed to Brazil first with the next group of missionaries and Bill was told he must stay in Ulster for a year to gain more experience in evangelistic work. They were thrilled at being accepted but the decision to send them at separate times stunningly disappointing. The couple must have thought, "If we are accepted for the work, why the delay, why the separation?"

It was a struggle to accept the mission ruling. Had not the Lord promised to "withhold no good thing from those that walk uprightly." If this were the case why then should Bill's dream be held back and their plans be sacrificed? Was this struggle a trial to see if he was willing to do the will of God?

A storm raged within Bill's heart until he finally came to the place of relinquishing his own will. The repeated lessons he had learned at college about self sacrifice and taking up his cross to follow Christ, were still fresh in his mind and now were becoming a reality in his life.

Life can often be a restless and disrupted experience until we surrender ourselves wholeheartedly to the will of God to follow and obey Him supremely. It is then that the Holy Spirit, Who performs many important ministries in our lives, gives us a calm and tranquil spirit, despite the adverse circumstances that may come our way.

The final meetings were completed, the barrels and metal trunks were all packed and it was with a heavy heart that Bill said farewell to his sweetheart at Belfast's Donegall Quay from where she sailed overnight to Liverpool. Although he was sad contemplating her departure, she was excited about the venture that lay ahead. The parting at the quayside did not help matters. Today the traveller departs in a moment with almost the immediacy of leaving one room to enter another and within hours is at his planned destination The pain of parting is quick, but composure is often regained by the time the passenger arrives in the departure lounge.

Forty years ago it was gangplanks, crowds at the quayside, the call "All aboard!" shrill whistles sounding and the untying of the moorings while the assembled crowd sang their favourite farewell hymns; "God be with you `til we meet again," or "Take the Name of Jesus with you." Often there was a seemingly endless delay before the boat, almost imperceptibly, began to separate from the dock and widen the gulf between the voyagers and those who came to say, sing and shout their farewells. The occasion was looked on as a Christian witness and often fellow passengers would enquire from the missionaries why there was so much singing.

The voices on the quayside continued to strain in song as handkerchiefs were waved in farewell. Slowly the departing missionaries drifted and disappeared down the Belfast Lough. Bill returned home that night comforted by the thought that he would be the next to sail to Brazil and be united with the one he loved. He promised to see her in Brazil within a year.

In Liverpool she boarded the SS Hilary. Early the next day Bill learned that their first port of call was to be Dublin, one hundred miles from Belfast. To be there for the ship's arrival Bill took the train south to the Irish capital to enjoy a final day with his sweetheart before she finally left on the long voyage to the sunnier climes of South America.

Bill had already proposed to this special girl and she had accepted. They would marry in Brazil. That was the plan. In Dublin he wanted to make their commitment to each other more official and secure their relationship with an engagement ring. Bill was disappointed that she was hesitant and preferred to leave it until he joined her in Brazil.

The train journey back to Belfast seemed endless. Sometimes Bill prayed and other times he tried to rationalise how it would all work out. A year seemed a long time but other things were already planned for him.

Chapter Eight

North Antrim

❖

For Bill's extra year of training the mission secretary had arranged with the Faith Mission that he should work for a year with one of their pilgrims under the leadership of Mr. Black in Ballymena in the North Antrim District. Willie Magee from Portadown was the pilgrim chosen to be Bill's co-worker. It proved to be a very rewarding partnership and a profitable time of evangelistic activity.

Missioning with the Faith Mission was not just a matter of conducting meetings. A lot of ground work had to be done. Willie and Bill organised days and even nights of prayer for the district. Much time was spent visiting the homes and farms in this rural area of Northern Ireland. The first district they went to was Ballynagarvey, a town near Ballymoney.

Mrs. Steele of Finvoy kindly provided them with hospitality at the family farmhouse from September until December of 1959. Bill already had friends at the nearby Cabra Free Presbyterian Church and he was glad to see the familiar faces when they came and supported the meetings. The various Faith Mission Prayer Unions in the area also attended the mission and brought visitors each night. The two evangelists preached on alternate nights for three months.

The gospel meetings started in the harvest season. The spiritual harvest was rich and rewarding for God blessed their work. When the mission finally terminated just before Christmas there was great reason for it to be a happy season, for many people had trusted the Saviour during the previous months.

One notable conversion as a result of the mission was that of a young man named Tommy Scott. He had attended the mission and God clearly spoke to him about sin and salvation. He was not converted at the meetings but back in his home he sought the Lord and asked the Saviour into his heart In later years Tommy went to train at the Faith Mission Bible College in Edinburgh, Scotland, and from there he also went to southern Brazil where he and his wife Margaret are still serving the Lord with OMS International.

Even though Bill was fully occupied with the evangelistic activities of the Faith Mission he was prayerfully following the progress of his girlfriend's voyage to Brazil and missing her greatly. He was hungry for her news. Everyday he waited for a letter but for five weeks there was nothing. He was certain news would arrive soon.

One morning while Bill was preparing a sermon for the evening meeting he was reading in Isaiah 37. The chapter relates the story of Sennacherib, the King of Ninevah, defying God and making his threats against King Hezekiah and against Jerusalem. He sent King Hezekiah a letter giving an ultimatum, either surrender the Holy City or the armies of Assyria would invade, kill the people and take Jerusalem by force. Militarily Hezekiah was greatly outnumbered and feared the worst. Hezekiah consulted Isaiah who encouraged the King to take the matter to God in prayer.

In his reading Bill got to verse 14 which reads, "And Hezekiah received the letter from the hand of the messengers, and read it: and Hezekiah went up unto the house of the Lord, and spread it before the Lord, and Hezekiah prayed unto the Lord."

Just at that point Mrs. Steele called from downstairs, "Bill, a letter has arrived for you." The kind Mrs. Steele was aware that Bill had been looking for mail everyday and she was as excited as Bill that something had finally arrived for him. However, Bill felt a strange sensation of foreboding and coincidence that he should be reading about Hezekaih receiving a disquieting letter centuries before just at the very moment when Mrs. Steele called.

The letter carried a Belfast post mark. His premonition gave him a sense of unease so he took the still unopened envelope to his bedroom. Before he opened the correspondence he did what he had learned Hezekiah had done with his letter, he spread it before the Lord. He prayed and asked the Lord for guidance and grace. The letter was short, curt and to the point, just half a page. The news was shattering. The words cut deeply like a knife into his heart. Nothing could have prepared Bill for this. The one he loved, considered to be his sweetheart and hopefully his future wife, wanted to end their relationship as she felt she no longer loved Bill.

Although he had been concerned about the prolonged absence of any correspondence he was unsuspecting of any change that might have taken place and was totally unprepared for a broken romance. Why this? Why me? Why now? were only a few of the questions that spun through Bill's mind and ripped his heart apart.

Tearfully Bill poured all his heartbreak out before the Lord. Even though confused and bewildered he felt the reassurance of God's voice through His Word which had brought unnatural peace to his troubled heart. He was to discover that disappointments are often God's instruments to build character for it is God who works in us both to will and do His good pleasure. At times it is hard to remember this when assailed by adversity.

The shock of the letter obviously shook Bill's sense of call. Could he proceed with his present plans and continue in preparation for going to Brazil? Friends at his home church were sympathetic and sensitive to the turmoil in which he found himself. Some accorded blame to different parties. Bill was careful not to become bitter because of this personal hurt. Others advised him to forget Brazil and remain in Ulster where he would undoubtedly have been in demand as a minister in his denomination.

Amid the many voices and much advice, Bill remembered the extraordinary and convincing way God had called him to Brazil and to the work of Acre Gospel Mission. He had learned to walk by faith based on the promises of God and he refused to wallow in self pity. He would not turn back.

From Ballynagarvey Bill and Willie Magee moved to the Craigs Mission Hall between Rasharkin and Garvagh. This move also involved a change of residence. Like the Steele family in Finvoy, the Barkley family at the Craigs not only gave them hospitality but treated them like part of the family.

Again the ground work had to be done; prayer meetings had to be organised; homes had to be visited, and the meetings conducted. The evangelistic mission at the Craigs Mission Hall lasted from early January until Easter of 1960. When God is blessing and people are trusting the Saviour, three months does not seem like a long time. Bill and Willie enjoyed great freedom in preaching and again scores of people were saved.

The months spent on missions in these locations were not without incident. On one occasion Bill was left with the responsibility of preparing the Mission Hall for the evening service. Besides tidying the Hall and making sure it was ready, he had to light the fire in the pot belly stove in the middle of the Hall. This was the only means of heating on the cold winter nights. Bill put paper and sticks into the old stove and tried to light the fire. His efforts were futile for the paper and sticks would not ignite. Bill decided to douse the paper and sticks with paraffin oil. He then opened the stove and threw in a match.

Before he could pull back a sudden burst of flames leaped up around him. In an instant he had lost his eye lashes and his eye brows. When he looked in the mirror to survey the damage he found that his forehead had gained an inch or more as the front of his hair had been singed by the fire! For several days Bill sent Willie out to do the visiting and preaching on his own while He conveniently stayed at home and prayed. He was too embarrassed to appear in public.

On Bill's first outing after this incident Willie Magee borrowed Harry McCloy's car for a visit to the Steeles up in Finvoy. With Bill in the passenger seat, Willie drove the van as hard as it would go along the narrow country roads. Because it was winter, the road was icy and when Willie tried to negotiate a bend on the narrow road he had to swerve to miss an oncoming car which was driven by another good friend, the late Billy McAuley. In trying to evade the other vehicle Willie veered the car to the left and in doing so he hit the bank on his near side, careered across the road and hit the verge on the other side after which the van rolled over and came to rest on its side. Although Harry's car was badly damaged the engine was still running. The two men were greatly shaken but neither injured.

"It's not the first car I've couped," said Willie Magee. The boys and Billy McAuley lifted the car unto its four wheels and Willie Magee lost no time in putting the car into first gear and sped off as if nothing had happened. Willie's driving greatly helped Bill's prayer life. It taught him to pray with his eyes open.

After Easter Bill and Willie moved on to Maboy Mission Hall just outside Portglenone and not too far away from the Craigs. Fresh ground had to be broken by doing the spade work of visiting, inviting, praying and preparing to preach. The evangelistic mission at Maboy, like the previous missions, lasted for almost three months finishing in June 1960. Again Bill and Willie were greatly used by God in that district and many local residents trace their conversion to those meetings.

While the evangelistic missions were in progress Bill was also preparing for his planned departure to Brazil at the end of that summer. Deputation meetings had to be fitted in, equipment was ordered from the tropical suppliers in London and baggage dispatched, injections and vaccines had to be taken and final visits to friends all had to be fitted in.

The late Pastor Willie Mullen was the guest speaker at the Acre Gospel Mission's Farewell Service for Bill in Belfast's central Wellington Hall on a fine summer's evening. His text was taken from the Palm Sunday account of our Lord's entry into Jerusalem. With typical humour becoming of Bill, Pastor Mullen spoke of the donkey and related the animal as a parallel to the outgoing missionary. "The Lord hath need of Him," said the Pastor. The preacher pointed out that like the donkey Bill was selected by the Lord for he

was chosen, sat on by the Lord for he was controlled and served the
Lord for he took Christ to the crowds. The parallels were obvious.
Well might the congregation have sung in farewell;

Oh Zion haste, thy mission high fulfilling,
To tell to all the world that God is Light,
That He who made all nations is not willing
One soul should perish, lost in shades of night.

Give of thy sons to bear the message glorious;
Give of thy wealth to speed them on their way;
Pour out thy soul for them in prayer victorious;
And all thou spendest Jesus will repay.

Chapter Nine

Bon Voyage

❖

The summer of 1959 saw Ulster locked in a series of industrial strikes. For a while there were no buses on the streets, no bread in the shops, no trains left the station, no dockers at Donegal Quay to unload the ships; even the weather was not great.

I remember it, for on 20th August that year I was present with a large group of people from Bill's home church and other friends who gathered at Belfast harbour to see Bill off. Because of the docker's strike we were not allowed near to the quay to see the Liverpool boat depart. Bill was glad he would possibly avoid the protracted agony that usually accompanied those dockside farewells, for his mother and sister planned to sail with him to Liverpool. Howbeit, Mr. Paisley, not to be out done from having a good farewell for the departing missionary, conducted an impromptu open-air meeting from the top of a wooden crate outside the terminal.

Surrounded by stacked up wooden containers and metal drums we sang "Take the Name of Jesus with You" to encourage God's servant leaving his native shore. As Bill finally departed toward the ship's gang plank there were shouts of farewell, and others called out Bible promises. It was a moving occasion. Before we dispersed we sang the customary "God be with be with you `til we meet again."

The ship loosed from her moorings and smoothly slipped out of the Donegal Quay. Being a fine summer's evening Bill and his sister stayed on deck as the ship sailed down Belfast Lough. On the southern shore Bill and Nina saw the receding Castlereagh Hills where he had spent part of his childhood at Ballygowan. They passed the little village of Holywood and the favourite holiday town of Bangor before entering the Irish Sea. Soon Ulster's coastline receded from view.

After supper with his mother and sister Bill retired to his cabin for the overnight crossing of the Irish Sea. He reflected on the friends who had gathered to see him off and was glad to be reassured that the Lord was with Him. As he lay on the bunk bed his mind drifted to and fro with the gentle roll of the vessel. He recalled how he had sailed through some rough waters and troubled seas since he first stepped out in obedience to God's call. All of that was history. What lay ahead was his uppermost concern. Suddenly the thought struck him that he could sleep safely in his cabin because he knew the captain was on the bridge, the ship's master was at the wheel. So also Bill rested in the knowledge that his Heavenly Captain was at the controls of his life. Jesus Christ is the Master of the waves and knew the uncharted seas of his life. Bill had a good night's sleep in the complete confidence that all his future was under the Master's control.

After a few days holiday in England with Nina and his mother, Bill returned to Liverpool where final good-byes were said to his family on board the ship. The SS Hubert, a sister ship of the SS Hilary, was an ocean going liner. It made the Liverpool ferry in which Bill had crossed from Belfast, look small. It was hard to imagine that a ship this size would travel a thousand miles up the Amazon River to Manaus, which was Bill's destination. The voyage would take six weeks and call at a number of ports en route. Bill intended to enjoy the journey.

Other missionaries boarded the ship with Bill. One couple was going to the UFM headquarters in Belem, Brazil. A single girl was going out to Trinidad to be married to her fiance who was a Church of England curate. The fellowship was good, the food was excellent, and needless to say, there was some fun with the missionary contingent.

In spite of the ship's apparent luxury nothing could ease the sea sickness of a passenger on his first time sailing through the swells of the Bay of Biscay. Bill's cabin was one of a series on a lower deck where he occupied an upper berth. In the middle of the night an old Portuguese man had obviously got up and gone to the bathroom because he was feeling sick. Unfortunately for Bill the old man lost his way on the return journey to his cabin. He mistook Bill's cabin for his own. When the man climbed to the upper berth and found it already occupied by another body be began to shout and yell in Portuguese. Bill, wakened out of sleep by the intruder in the dark, also began to shout back in English. Neither could understand the other.

Once he was able to oust the man from his cabin Bill made sure that for the rest of the trip he slept behind locked doors. In the dark he couldn't see the man's face, nor the man his, so he was never able to single out who the midnight prowler had been but hoped he would disembark at the next port which was Lisbon. The incident was never repeated.

Another mishap awaited Bill and his friends in Lisbon. The ship docked for several hours during which time the passengers were allowed ashore. The missionary group headed off to the zoo and from there to the city centre. It had been a great day, but soon it was time to return to the ship before it sailed. Bill and the curate's fianceé had become separated from the other couple and decided to take a taxi back to the boat. They couldn't find a driver who spoke English so Bill put his English/Portuguese dictionary to good use and looked up the word for "boat," "ship" and "harbour" until eventually they made themselves understood — so they hoped.

The taxi driver whisked them through Lisbon's busy streets and frantic traffic, weaving in and out past the electric trams. Nothing seemed familiar or indicated they were getting nearer to the docks.

Fearing they were going to miss the boat and doubtful if that was where the man was taking them, Bill tapped the driver on the shoulder and with open dictionary tried to pronounce the word for "stop." When the driver finally stopped they paid the fare and got out of the taxi. Bill began to panic as he imagined what would happen if they missed the boat and he was stranded with the curate's fiance in Portugal. There would need to be some explaining done both to the mission back home and to an angry cleric in the West Indies.

They stopped a police man who spoke some English and to their relief he said he would call a taxi and send them in the right direction. The police officer stepped into the busy road and called the first taxi that passed. Some heated discussion took place between the officer and the driver. Bill and the girl were aghast when the policeman said, "This driver said he was already taking you to the port when you insisted on stopping and now you want to go again." Meekly, Bill and the girl got into the taxi and not a word was spoken all the way to the boat.

The long days and clear nights of the ocean crossing were just the sort of rest Bill needed. He swam in the swimming pool which was constantly replenished with sea water. He watched the flying fish skip over the waves and the dolphins dance as they escorted the ship on its journey through the Caribbean. Besides Lisbon, the ship took Bill to such exotic places as the beautiful Portuguese island of Madeira, Barbados, and Trinidad where they said farewell to the bride to be. It was then onto Belem at the mouth of the Amazon River. In those days it seemed that only millionaires and missionaries could enjoy such a cruise. During the crossing of the Atlantic there were opportunities to witness to passengers and to preach at the Sunday Services on board the ship and then again at churches in Barbados and Trinidad.

Ted Laskowski, Field Leader of UFM Brazil, came to meet the new missionaries at Belem. This was Bill's first experience of Brazil, and it felt good to finally set foot in the land to which God had called him. After a warm welcome by the friends at the UFM base it was back to the boat which had docked for only four hours.

It was an awesome experience to see the large ship being navigated through the narrows of the delta which encircle the large island of Marajo situated at the mouth of the mighty Amazon. The lush green and dense forest on either side seemed to be so near. People waved and gestured from their riverside dwellings, and little boys came out in dug-out canoes to pick up gifts of bread and other items that passengers threw to them. The same canoes danced up and down in the huge waves of muddy brown water left in the wake of the great vessel. Overhead, large black vultures floated motionless in the air waiting to swoop on any carrion that might catch their beady eyes.

After five days on the Amazon the ship finally entered the Rio Negro and then steamed up river to berth at the floating dock at Manaus. Bill had finally arrived.

Chapter Ten

Everything's New

❖

One hundred years ago Manaus was the richest city in Latin America. Tram cars ran on the city's main street, the Avenida Eduardo Ribeiro, before they ran on the streets of Belfast or Liverpool. "Black Gold" was the nickname given to the raw rubber latex which was in great demand all over the world, and the Amazon region was its prime source. The financial investment in the region was responsible for the development of French, English and Portuguese communities.

Today the vestige of the former economic boom remains. The floating dock was first built by the British; the lovely Custom House was constructed with sandstone imported from Scotland. The famous Amazon Theatre, graced by the Great Caruso and more recently the Spanish tenor, Jose Carreras, boasts of marble brought from Italy and exquisite murals painted by the best Italian artists at the end of the last century. Most of the older houses bear the characteristics of Portuguese architecture with tall windows, high ceilings and ornate designs embossed on the exterior.

Manaus is situated in the heart of Amazonas and is all the more remarkable because it is a virtual island in the jungle. In 1997 there are still no roads linking the city to the rest of Brazil. All importing and exporting to and from the city is conducted by river or by air. The scores of tributaries that flow into the Amazon form the vital arteries of life for the people who live in the surrounding forest. Merchant men travel in all sizes of brightly painted boats up and down the river selling their wares in small towns and at the river edge. In return they buy Brazil nuts, rubber latex or wood for foreign export or salted fish and fruit for the local market.

The day the SS Hubert docked at Manaus in 1960 with Bill on board, a group of missionaries and Brazilian friends came down to welcome the new arrival. These included Fred Orr who had come down from Labrea, and Bill Barkley, an Ulster missionary who worked with the West Amazon Mission.

There were only two conventional cars in Manaus at that time. All other transport was by jeep because of the precarious state of the roads. A jeep was hired to transport Bill, his baggage and the friends to Bill Barkley's apartment which would be Bill Wood's residence in Manaus for the next few weeks. The heat and the humidity of Manaus were overwhelming. Tropical trees lined avenues; the cacophony of street traders and the babble of a strange tongue, plus the smell of roasted coffee and other unidentifiable odours gave Bill his first taste of culture shock.

This shock was emphasised to Bill when on the day after he arrived he was taken to a small restaurant near to Bill Barkley's apartment. The restaurant had the peculiar and suspicious distinction of being named The Black Cat. In spite of any doubts Bill might have had about the name of the restaurant, the food was good and the black cat was not on the menu. Fred had ordered for Bill on that first day and had called the dish by its Portuguese name. Bill enjoyed the meal, and he asked Fred how to pronounce the name of it. Frustratingly for Bill he had the same meal everyday for the next four weeks—it was the only food he knew how to order.

Attendance at the local Regular Baptist Church was an experience. The welcome was warm, and the atmosphere was even hotter and a bit more sticky. Beyond the usual handshake that Bill was used to came the good Brazilian hug and a slap on the back. The newcomer always feels a bit awkward how to go about this embrace, and of course, he must learn it is only men with men. There was no piano nor organ to lead the hymns, but in good Latin style a few guitars were strummed. The hymns had familiar tunes, obviously translated from English, but the strange sounding words were hard to pronounce, and making the words keep up with the music was just too much.

During those first few weeks Bill drank in the atmosphere as well as gallons of fruit juices and a local drink called Guarana. This is a very pleasant soft drink made from a fruit peculiar to the Amazon. He tasted and enjoyed the savour of many new fruits which included cupuacu, graviola, mamao, maracuja and he fell in love with acai.

The siesta was another custom to which Bill had no trouble adapting—it took him about twenty-four hours to get used to it. In the midday heat of the tropical sun the shops closed, and the streets virtually cleared of people. After lunch most people retired to their bed or hammock for an hour of rest. Bill was told that if he wanted to enjoy good health in the tropics he should always respect this local custom. He took to it like a duck to water.

While resting at siesta time Bill not only recalled how the Lord had guided him, provided for him and now brought him to this land so far from home. He pondered the future. Where would he work? When would he ever be ready to preach? Would God use him here as he had used him in North Antrim? Bill wanted to be a soul winner and a church planter — God's instrument in this land.

Bill's first letter home for publication in the Acre Gospel Mission News Letter reads:

It must be with a note of praise that I write this first letter for the circular. The Psalmist said, "The Lord hath done great things for us whereof we are glad"- and I would echo his words of praise to the Almighty. Let me share with you some of the things He hath done on my behalf.

It was on the 20th July, 1952 that the Lord did the greatest thing of all for me; brought salvation to my darkened heart.

Amazing Grace, how sweet the sound
That saved a wretch like me,
I once was lost but now am found,
Was blind but now I see.

It was after sitting for three months under the ministry of Dr. Ian Paisley that I accepted Jesus Christ. How I praise the Lord for that night when I became a new creature in Christ, and He became my personal Friend and Saviour.

In the years that followed I was often found in missionary meetings and conventions but never dreamed that the Lord would want me to take the Gospel to those that sit far off in darkness. The first missionary that I heard speaking after I was converted was Miss Mollie Harvey, and although my heart was stirred by the message that she gave, much of which I can remember to this day, yet would have seemed ridiculous if I had been told that one day I should join the work of which she spoke. It was through a meeting at which Mrs. Jesse Eades, a missionary from the Cape Verde Islands, West Africa, was the speaker and through the home call of Mrs. Ina Orr en route for Boca do Acre in Brazil that I was challenged to yield my life to the Lord's control.

From there the Lord led me to spend two years in the Missionary Training College of the Worldwide Evangelisation Crusade. Precious years were they — I could never tell you all the Lord did for me during that time. But it was there as I sought the Lord as to where my future field of service should be, that He directed me to the Acre Gospel Mission. As I left the MTC at the end of my training there, the promise that the Lord gave me was, "Behold I have set before thee an open door which no man can shut."

Before that door opened there was a Missionary Candidates Course to be taken and seven months of evangelistic work with the Faith Mission in County Antrim, Northern Ireland. During these months it was a great joy to point many souls to the One who "is able to save to uttermost." On August 21st in the midst of the Seamen's strike when hundreds of sailings were cancelled, the Lord overruled and the RMS Hubert on which I was booked to sail on

August 19th, left for Brazil. The voyage to Brazil was interesting and pleasant. The Lord gave many opportunities to witness: twice in Sunday services on the ship, in a Baptist Church in Barbados, and also in three meetings in Trinidad I had opportunity to preach the Gospel.

And now here I am in Brazil — at the moment of writing in the town of Manaus — 1,000 miles up the River Amazon. Fred Orr was here to meet me when I arrived, and now we are preparing to journey into the interior. How happy I am to be here in this very needy valley of Amazonas and how conscious of being in the centre of God's will. Pray that the Lord will enable me in the study of the language and that soon I may have the joy of pointing scores of these dear Brazilians to the Saviour. Hallelujah!

While Bill contemplated and speculated about the future, he knew he could be of little use as a missionary without first learning Portuguese. The decision was made that he should go to Labrea to study the language with Fred Orr.

The initial trip to Labrea was a memorable experience. Eighteen passengers climbed up the steps and then descended into the body of the aircraft, a Catalina Seaplane belonging to Pan Air, one of Brazil's national airlines. After accelerating down the runway, they were soon climbing above Manaus and into the blue sky. The roar of the two engines was deafening. Looking below Bill got a good view of Manaus, the colonial buildings, the harbour, the floating city of makeshift dwellings, scores of boats moored along the river's edge and the vast network of waterways that meandered through what looked like virgin jungle. As the plane gained altitude, small white clouds below the aircraft grouped together like fluffy flocks of sheep on a green carpet of grass which the Creator had rolled out over the Amazon Valley.

After almost three hours flight, the plane began its descent toward Canutama on the River Purus. At the extremes of the Catalina's wings the floats lowered for landing on the river. When the tail of the plane touched the muddy brown water there was an almost unbearably loud roar as if the metal fuselage were being ripped apart. Bill was convinced his life in Brazil was going to be a short span only and they were all heading for a watery grave. Fred assured him this was normal, and he would soon get used to it.

Canoes came out to meet the aircraft, and some passengers disembarked into them. The passengers were given shade from the scorching sun under the canopy of a black umbrella while the boatman paddled towards the river bank. As the plane slowly drifted downstream, other passengers for Labrea and Boca do Acre climbed aboard and filled the empty seats. If the landing had been fearful, Bill was now fascinated to see what the take-off would be like.

The hatch was closed; canoes paddled clear of the propellers, and soon the engines started. When the engines got to full throttle the craft was shuddering; suddenly the Catalina surged forward and began to cut its way through the water with gathering speed. Huge waves fanned out in its wake. Before long the craft lifted off from the water, and they were airborne again. The floats at the end of the wings automatically folded away. Soon they were once more speeding up through the clouds.

The flight had given Bill plenty of material to write about to his brother Brian who was serving as a navigator with the RAF.

When the aircraft drew into the river's edge at Labrea, Bill emerged from the plane with Fred to find a group of local believers along with missionary Allen Loney standing on the river bank ready to welcome the new missionary. Ladies stood under the shade given by a few flimsy umbrellas, and for the same purpose, many of the men wore straw hats. There followed the now familiar Brazilian hugs and some unintelligible words of greetings. Bill replied with a few words in Portuguese he had picked up in Manaus.

Jose Pinheiro, a local dentist and photographer trained in both trades by Allen Loney, took photographs to record the occasion. Luiz Marinho, a deacon in the church, stretched out his arms to Bill and with great gusto spoke some unintelligible words in Portuguese. Fred came to Bill's rescue and interpreted what Luiz had been saying, "I have nothing to offer by way of money or material, but here are my two arms to serve you whenever you need my help."

After the initial greetings the party of missionaries and Brazilians made their way up the river bank, across the town square and along the street to the mission house where a welcome cold drink was ready for everyone. Fred Orr wrote home of Bill's arrival, "Bill had a great welcome here in Labrea, and I am sure he will not easily forget the precious promises from God's Word given to him by the believers here. We have language study every day, and once again the Lord is answering all your prayers. Bill is making swift progress and will soon be taking part in the work."

Another episode happened to Bill on arrival in Labrea. Before leaving Belfast he had been advised by James Gunning the field leader who was on furlough, to take a good Panama hat out with him to give him adequate shade from the hot sun. Bill ordered the hat from the tropical suppliers in London. It came well packed, but to ensure that it was not damaged on the journey, Bill had carried the bag containing the hat all the way from Belfast to Brazil, thankfully without incident on the journey. In Manaus he did not feel he needed to wear the straw hat so he decided to carry it still in the bag as hand luggage on the flight to Labrea. When they got to the mission house, many believers wanted to shake Bill's hand. Not to inhibit the hand shakes Bill set the bag containing the hat on a chair. Once he had finished the various greetings he decided to sit down, and did so — on top of the hat. He never did get wearing the hat on his head. The posterior part of his anatomy wore it out on the first day.

The town of Labrea is located on the southern bank of the Rio Purus, one thousand five hundred miles from the mouth of the Amazon River and is one of its main tributaries. The town was named after a famous explorer of the surrounding forests, Colonel Labrea, and is built around the large main square, the dominating feature of which is the Catholic church. In 1960 cars had not yet arrived in Labrea. Transport in town was either by bullock, bicycle, horse or on foot. Transport on the river was mostly by dugout canoes or on the larger boats that coursed up and downstream.

It had been over six years since Fred and Ina Orr as new missionaries had arrived in the small port at the bend on the river. Ina had never placed a foot in Labrea, for within a short while of the steamer's arrival Ina had passed into the presence of her Lord.

The shock was felt in Christian circles around the world. Subsequent to Ina's death Fred went to Boca do Acre and later returned to Labrea with James and Dorrie Gunning. In spite of opposition in the town, a non-Christian Syrian immigrant friend gave Fred a large piece of land near to the town centre. Over the course of the next few years James helped Fred construct a house on the site, and Allen Loney was there to lend his skills for the finishing touches to the building. Ample room was made on the veranda for those early meetings. The first few years required a lot of plodding work from Fred and the other missionaries who came to help. Soon the church was founded.

When Bill looked around at the believers who had come to welcome him, he could not help but think of the price that had been paid to bring the Gospel to this town. The corn of wheat had already died, now this was the spiritual harvest.

A few days after his arrival Bill went with Fred and Allen to the cemetery on the outskirts of town to visit Ina's grave. There he read the words, "I have glorified Thee on earth, I have finished the work Thou gavest me to do." (John 17:4) In reverent stillness Bill bowed his head, and bearing in mind the sacrifice paid, remembering that through the death of this young woman God had called him to Brazil, he rededicated his life to Jesus Christ. Well might Bill have remembered the words of Margaret Clarkson's hymn:

So send I you to labour unrewarded,
To serve unpaid, unloved, unsought, unknown,
To bear rebuke, to suffer pain and scoffing -
So send I you to suffer for My sake.

So send I you to leave your life's ambition,
To die to dear desire, self will resign,
To labour long and love where men revile you -
So send I you to lose your life in Mine.

As the Father has sent Me, so send I you.

Bill later said, "Now that I had arrived at the place where God had sent me and for which I had often prayed and over a long period prepared, I felt frustrated. Everyone wanted to speak to me, but I was up against the language barrier, and I knew that this was the first hurdle I would have to cross." If there were frustration in not being able to speak Portuguese, Bill was soon to find out there would be even greater frustrations learning how to speak this new language.

After the first few days in Labrea Bill settled down to classes every morning at the mission house. Bill was soon wrestling with nasalized vowels, diphthongs, "r" pronounced as though it were an "h"; Bill also had to know when an "h" was silent or when it was pronounced like a "y." His head was swimming with the conjugations of verbs in all their different tenses, persons and conditions.

Armed with all this learning, he attempted to put sentences together and practice on willing and patient listeners either at the church or while visiting homes. Of course, like everyone who learns a foreign language, there were not only the usual blunders and mistakes; some of them were positively embarrassing.

One day Bill needed to buy batteries for his flashlight. Not sure of how he should ask for batteries he wrote the request on a piece of paper. "Do you have any batteries?" If the reply were in the affirmative, then he wanted to ask for six. On the way to the store Bill tried to memorise the question, "O senhor tem pilhas?" (Sir, do you have batteries.) The problem was that Bill failed to decipher his own hand writing and mistook the "p" of pilha for "f" thus changing it to "filha" which is the Portuguese word for daughter. You can imagine the surprise on the amused owner's face when in reply to the young missionary's enquiry if he had any daughters, he answered "Yes." To this Bill requested, "I would like to buy six of them please."

As Bill became more fluent in Portuguese, he became more aware of people's needs and problems. He visited the homes and got to know family backgrounds. It was in Labrea he had to become accustomed to his new name. "Bill" sounded too much like an imported name, so he adopted the name "Guilhereme," and by this name he is still known all over Brazil.

With Fred, Allen and the believers he ventured up river and then down river by canoe to conduct meetings in the palm leaf covered homes at the water edge. Within a short time Bill was plunged into the deep end of regular church activities using his Portuguese and was expected to preach at the church meetings. He remembered the day at Ormeau Park when he had been invited to speak in public for the first time and had tried to run from the microphone. He had come a long way since then, and the Lord had greatly helped him with the Portuguese language.

In the course of visitation he got to know Geraldo who cared for the garden of the mission property. On Sunday afternoons a group from the church went to visit him. Geraldo lived in a very simple dwelling in a little clearing of forest removed some distance from the main hub of the town. His simple home, where he lived alone, was made of palm wood walls and floors and had a palm leaf covering. It was purposely built in isolation because Geraldo had leprosy. On being diagnosed a few years earlier, his wife had abandoned him because of the disease. Missionaries and believers had befriended him and supported him as much as they could.

Unknown to Bill, his meeting with Geraldo was an indication of things to come. This was the first person Bill had ever met who had leprosy. He could never have known in his wildest dreams that in future years he would operate on Geraldo to amputate his leg and do other surgery to help correct his vision.

God answers our prayers and the prayers of others, by doing far more than we can ever imagine.

Chapter Eleven

On The Move

❖

A white Christmas in Boca do Acre is as rare as a tropical heat wave in the Arctic Circle. Mollie Harvey, the veteran missionary whom Bill had met at the Ravenhill Free Presbyterian Church years previously, had invited him to spend Christmas in Boca do Acre. Bill ventured again onto the Catalina plane for the almost two hour flight from Labrea to the Boca which was a further 500 miles up river.

Boca do Acre was basically composed of two long streets each of which was about a mile long, and both terminated abruptly at either end at the forest's edge. The streets ran from east to west, and this meant that the brilliant sunlight beat down mercilessly on the two streets from sun up to sundown making it one of the hottest towns in the Amazon Valley. Like Labrea and the other interior towns, there was only one small generator in the town which gave electricity to the streets and houses for three hours every evening from 6:00 to 9:00 p.m..

There were no Christmas trees available in Boca do Acre, but palm branches were suitably decorated with strips of coloured crepe paper and match boxes covered in silver wrapping. Cotton wool was a poor substitute for pristine snow, but this was enhanced by silver glitter which helped create a festive atmosphere. Christmas cards from friends at home decked a panel on the wall of the mission house.

In the kitchen further preparation was made with a cake baked from the precious ration of dried fruit which had been brought from home. Bananas took the place of apples in baking tarts, and tinned margarine was brought from Manaus to make the traditional shortbread. The main course ran unsuspectingly around the back garden contentedly scratching and pecking. All the goodies had to be stored in some place out of reach of the ever present armies of ants that attacked anything that was left exposed. The safest place to store the prepared food was in a small kerosene fridge which had recently been acquired by Mollie.

Daily rehearsals were held at the church for the Christmas programme. It seemed strange to listen to the firm Christmas favourites such as"O Come all ye Faithful" and "Away in a Manger" not only sung in another tongue, but echoing from the simple wooden church building and not a drop of snow in sight. Definitely not the weather for singing "See Amid the Winter Snow."

The Christmas party was a treat to attend. Bill was now more proficient in Portuguese and had ample opportunity for preaching at the various meetings. Those who organised the party took advantage of Bill; they decked him in a mock-up Santa suit, and he played the role of Santa to the children. Kind friends from home sent little dolls for the girls and small cars for the boys so everyone got something. On Christmas Eve the long awaited and rehearsed Christmas programme was performed. The church was packed to capacity with parents and friends who came to hear the boys and girls tell the story of the Saviour's birth by their readings, verse and song .

On Christmas morning the chickens were in the oven early, and Mollie was in full control of preparing the Christmas meal. At the table there was a time of good fun and fellowship and then time to think of their families back home and exchange stories of what they might be doing just then. It was a way of releasing any homesickness that is often felt at Christmas. The day was a time to relax after all the pre-Christmas preparations and activities.

A field conference was planned in Labrea at the beginning of January, and everyone was looking forward to it. Some of the missionaries were on furlough, and that depleted the numbers to six. From Bill's point of view the most memorable thing to come out of that first conference was the decision to send him to work with Jack and Joan Mawdsley at Canutama.

The Mawdsleys, from Liverpool, had met the Mayor of Canutama on an internal flight several years previously. He invited them to his town to establish an evangelical work. They accepted the invitation and ventured into what was virgin soil for the Gospel. Initially there was a ready response and quite a few accepted the Saviour. In spite of opposition from a local Spanish priest, land was purchased in the centre of town and a church building was erected. A local trader who lived in Manaus, Senhor Milton Rosa, a very zealous believer, made his house in Canutama available for the missionaries.

By the time Bill arrived the work was almost four years old. Canutama was smaller than Labrea and Boca do Acre, and it didn't take long for Bill to get to know the town and the people. He visited them in their homes and quickly established a rapport with many believers and unbelievers. Bill, now fluent in the language, shared the preaching every week with Jack Mawdsley.

Besides conducting the full programme of meetings and evangelistic activities in the town, Jack and Joan also travelled on a small boat to conduct evangelistic meetings up the surrounding tributaries. The Mensageiro da Paz (Messenger of Peace as it was called) was twenty-five feet long, five feet wide and was powered by an eight horse power Kelvin diesel engine imported from the United Kingdom. The boat chugged up and down the River Purus and other nearby tributaries bringing medical aid to those who needed it but primarily to spread the message of the Gospel in that region.

Writing for the mission circular in 1961 Bill reported:

Behind the darkest clouds there is always a ray of sunshine, and in the midst of hardness, opposition and indifference there are also many hungry hearts. We have been proving this during the last few weeks here in Canutama. Jack, Joan and I, as we labour together have been conscious of your prayers and of the Lord's presence with us—His good hand upon us; helping, guiding, blessing, saving—in the study of the language, in the building of the church, in the meetings and in general contact with the people. You can imagine how thrilled we were a few weeks ago when Jack received a letter asking to him hold a meeting in a house up river. The letter was from one of the most Catholic areas on the river, and how we praise the Lord for this open door.

A few days ago Jack and I happily set off in the Mensageiro da Paz travelling four hours up river. We arrived at the home to which we had been invited and were graciously received. The meeting was held in a large room, and it was soon packed with thirty to forty people. I played the accordion and Jack sang. I gave a word of testimony, and Jack gave the Gospel message. The attention and the interest were amazing. After the meeting many came forward with questions showing real interest in the things of God. I wonder when we will have the opportunity to go there again?

In the absence of any doctor or medical help Joan Mawdsely used her acquired medical and midwifery skills to treat many sick in the town and attend the confinement and delivery of numerous children. This was greatly appreciated considering the nearest access to a doctor was either three hours away by aeroplane which made irregular weekly visits or seven days on a boat down river to Manaus.

Jim Elliott, the American missionary martyred among the Auca Indians of Ecuador a few years earlier said, "Wherever you are, be all there. Live to the hilt in every situation you believe to be the will of God." Bill Woods had arrived at the place to which God had brought him. He wanted to "live to the hilt" in the will of God.

Bill found being able to preach in a foreign tongue to be greatly fulfilling, but the greatest encouragement and blessing occurred when people began to accept Christ as a result of his preaching. One outstanding case was that of a family that had recently arrived from their home up river at Nova Vista. This was a typical seringal, a centre from which workers fanned out into the forest to gouge the latex from the rubber trees. Senhor Walter and Dona Adelha felt they could no longer face the rigors of life in their isolated riverside home where within one month they had lost three children. They had been victims of a fever that had scourged the River Purus. Locally the disease was dubbed "the black fever" because of the black substance vomited by the patients at the latter stages of the illness just before death. Most of its victims were either children or adolescents. Sadly, Bill saw the ravages of this disease that had no known cure.

Dona Adelha had been sure to bring all her saints, and when the family arrived in town she gave them a prominent place in the house which the family had secured at the river front in Canutama. Periodic bouts of depression demented Dona Adelha, and often at nights she would flee into the forest and call the names of her departed children. When in these depressed moods she earnestly prayed to all the saints and even at times to Jesus. Her veneration to the saints did nothing to relieve her greatest fears and lift the depression, but when she called on the Name of Jesus she found peace.

She related her experience to a believer who invited Dona Adelha to the meetings at the Evangelical Church. She wrestled with what she had heard about Jesus Christ being able to save, forgive and give a new life. She could not turn her back on her saints to whom she had prayed nightly for many years.

Finally, one day while Bill visited the house, Adelha confessed in the presence of the family she could no longer continue in her old life. She needed Jesus Christ. Bill had the joy of showing her the simple way of salvation. The transformation was radical. Even as she broke her plaster saints she realised how vain her idolatry had been. She burned the fetishes she had previously and superstitiously embraced. Now she was a new person.

News of Adelha's conversion not only spread round the town quickly, but had an immediate impact on her family and, as was to develop later, a lasting impact on other parts of Amazonas. Her daughter Maria do Carmo trusted the Saviour a few years later. Bill performed the wedding ceremony in Canutama when Maria married Pastor Moacir who came to work as a seminary student with Bill. This couple have subsequently founded nine Baptist congregations in Manaus, and their son, Pastor Elieser, is presently pastoring the church in Canutama. Another son of Dona Adelha, Edson, is also an active preacher in Baptist churches in Manaus.

Bill's first experience of prolonged river evangelism took place when he accompanied Jack on a journey that lasted over one month. The trip took them several days down the River Purus, and then they entered into the River Tapuáwhich they navigated for some days before entering into yet another tributary, the River Cunhu. This was a pioneer trip, for missionaries had never coursed these waters before.

Beside Bill and Jack, there was old Joao, a believer from Canutama, who went along as a ready helper. All the food and fuel needed for a month had to be carried with them. Hopefully they would find people who would supply them with fresh fish or wild game killed in the forest. Cooking was done with Primus stoves on board the boat. They also had a wide variety of medicines to help treat any sick natives they might encounter. On board they were also well stocked with Gospel literature for distribution. At night they used hurricane lamps either for the meetings or to light up the boat, and hung their hammocks and draped them over with mosquito nets to try to get some sleep.

These pioneer meetings followed a regular pattern. Perhaps Capinrao was typical of most; arriving at the jungle clearing late in the afternoon, a visit was paid to the largest house. All of the dwellings were built on stilts because of flooding when the river overflowed its banks each rainy season. Most of the houses were covered with palm branches and floored with palm wood. Some houses had walls, but most were open except for a small enclosed bedroom. Livestock generally consisted of a few black pigs, an indefinite number of scrawny chickens and several dogs, all of which roamed freely around the clearing.

It was evident by the images on the walls that these people were nominal Catholics and yet in typical Brazilian cordiality, Senhor Sebastiao welcomed the missionaries to his home. When permission was asked for a meeting it was readily given.

In place of a much needed shower Bill and Jack bathed in the muddy waters of the river. After eating the staple food of rice and beans for supper they carried their hurricane lamps, literature and other necessary items up to Sebastiao's house, where the meeting was to be conducted. People gathered from the surrounding forest, and others came from the other side of the wide river.

Soon the improvised meeting place was filled with people sitting all over the floor, and others stood outside in the night air. The meeting got under way with Bill, Jack and old Joao singing a few hymns and choruses. The humid air and high temperatures caused streams of perspiration to course down their faces and backs while swarms of hungry mosquitoes and other pests flew around them and frequently fed on their exposed arms and ankles. The discomfort of the surroundings was balanced by the joy of bringing the Gospel to these people for the very first time.

At the end of that meeting Senhor Sebastiao accepted Jesus Christ as his Saviour. Like many others who lived in the isolation of the jungle he had a tragic story to tell of how he had recently lost his two teenage sons; in clear view of Sebastiao's house his two sons took a dug-out canoe across the river to visit friends who lived in a clearing at the other side. The father looked on helplessly from a distance when he saw a thirty foot long Anaconda snake push the canoe over and pull the youngest boy down into the muddy waters. The other son hurriedly swam to safety. The father and others rushed to their canoes and went in pursuit of the missing boy and the snake; neither were found.

Sebastiao's heart broke when the tragedy re-occurred a month later when the other teenage son, who had escaped the first close encounter with the feared Anaconda, suffered a similar fate. He was fishing in the middle of the river when suddenly he was pulled into the murky water, possibly by the same snake, and was never seen again. Sebastiao's heavy heart was fertile ground for the comfort of the Gospel, and Jack and Bill had the great joy of leading him to personal faith in Jesus Christ.

The experience of that meeting at Capinrao was repeated nightly for nearly a full month before the tired, happy and much slimmer missionaries returned to Canutama. Bill really enjoyed this work and gave himself wholly to it. He wrote of his work with Jack Mawdsley:

During the entire month of August our boat, O Mensageiro da Paz, chugged hundreds of miles on the river taking Jack and me with the message of the Gospel to many darkened and hungry hearts who live along the banks of the Rivers Tapau, Cunhuáand Ipiranha. Day after day we travelled on, ever going deeper into the interior, always meeting people who were eager to hear the Good News. In the very first home at which we stopped we found hearts that were prepared to receive the Saviour. The father had been reading to his family for some time from an old tattered Bible, and a few days before our arrival their hearts had been softened by the death of their son. It was thought that a huge snake pulled him into the river and he was never seen again.

Poverty and sickness abounded everywhere. I shall never forget going into one wee hut and climbing on my hands and knees under a thick mosquito net. When I got there I had to wait until the woman of the house brought a light, and eventually I was able to see her husband lying in a hammock. His leg was in such a rotten mess that I could not even begin to describe it—a snake had bitten him a few days beforehand. We gave him all the medicines we had, but that was only enough to start the treatment. Today I am still looking for someone going into that far flung place to take more medicine to him.

Eventually we navigated into a small stream and had to leave the boat and travel by canoe. Even then it was with great difficulty that the canoe was able to pass the obstacles on the narrow river. Often we had to get out of the canoe and haul it over fallen trees or cut our way through thick foliage that blocked our path. We rowed for eight days visiting the homes. It was our joy at the headwaters of this stream to visit a small tribe of Indians who live there in the depths of the forest. We do praise the Lord for His protection on the journey, but most of all we praise Him for at least four precious souls who trusted the Lord as their Saviour.

It seemed the Lord was preparing Bill's heart for a future that was still wholly unknown to him; suffering and death were to make a deep impression on his life and ministry. Writing home during that first year in Canutama he recounted:

One thing that has completely amazed me here is how quickly death comes to these jungles. With little or no warning a fever sets in, and in a few hours another life is gone. A little boy who lived just across the street from us suddenly became ill. On the fourth day of the illness the boy's screams and shouts could be heard on the street and it made my blood run cold. He died on the fifth day.

Recently, Jack, Joan and I decided to visit a young girl afflicted with leprosy who had been ill for some months. We travelled down river a short distance to her little shack of a house which was completely surrounded by the jungle. We found her lying in a hammock and learned that she had taken a turn for the worse during the previous night. We enquired what she had been eating. "That's just the problem," came the reply. "We have absolutely nothing to eat and have had nothing for days, not even coffee or milk to drink. We have been living on water." Within half an hour we returned to the poverty stricken house with some rice, milk and more medicines. Just as we stopped the boat at the river bank near to their house we could see a lighted candle on the floor and when the motor was turned off we could hear the mother wailing for her daughter who had just died. She was only seventeen years old and for six years had suffered from the terrible disease of leprosy. They were already planning to bury her just as she was, wrapped in her hammock, but they were very grateful when we suggested that one of the believers who is a carpenter would make a coffin from some of the wooden boards we were using for the new church. Sadly, for many here the battle for life is a losing one.

The physical suffering, the social poverty and the spiritual darkness seemed to be overwhelming challenges with which Bill wrestled to know how he could best be a faithful servant of Jesus Christ in the face of these tremendous needs.

Chapter Twelve

Heartache

❖

The end of the first year in Canutama was crowned with great joy when the newly built church opened. When not travelling on the rivers Jack and Bill busied themselves erecting the wooden building with the help of a few hired workers from the town. Bill wrote an account of the work in a letter home:

It hardly seemed possible! It was Christmas Eve and the new church building was at last ready for use. Jack and I stood looking round the church and the six forms wondering who was going to fill them later that evening for the opening meeting. Just to be on the safe side we borrowed a few more forms and a dozen chairs. "That will be plenty of seats now," I thought. Later that evening the crowds began to pour in. At first I thought my eyes were lying. Surely Mr. So and So could not be coming here and never did I think that he would ever be in a meeting never mind bring his whole family.

Before the time to start the meeting the church was packed, and it was then the fun began. I had to run up and down the street borrowing seats and forms for the extra people. At one house a group of visitors had just arrived and had just sat down for tea. When she heard our predicament the lady of the house ordered them all to their feet and pulled the old wooden bench from under them. Some of the most Catholic chairs and benches in Canutama were put to use in the meeting that night. It is little wonder the priest was mad. I counted over one hundred and fifty people seated, and another thirty stood in the aisle and another forty outside. There was rapt attention from all present, but near the end of the meeting the priest came down the street and ordered those who were standing outside to leave the meeting. At first no one budged. He then got madder, and one by one the overflow drifted away until only one woman was left standing. We were glad; the devil was sad; the priest was mad—Hallelujah!

When Jack and Joan left for home in February 1962 it was feared that the isolation and loneliness for Bill, a bachelor, would be too much. Those who were concerned need never have worried. Besides plenty of activity in the town, the house was always full. Work at the church in Canutama kept Bill busy, and new contacts were being made for the Gospel. A congregation had started in Reposo, a clearing in the jungle where the rubber workers lived. This was a one hour journey down river. Other opportunities were presented up river. Bill was immersed in the work and the months slipped by.

He was greatly encouraged to hear that James and Dorrie Gunning had returned from furlough and were working in Labrea while Fred Orr visited the North East. After a busy year in Canutama, Bill decided in June 1962 to take a break and visit Labrea.

When he arrived he was pleasantly surprised to find his former girlfriend was also in Labrea visiting James and Dorrie. Besides filling them in on all the news of the work and comparing notes of all that had happened since Bill had last seen James and Dorrie, there were also some heart-to-heart talks between the former sweethearts. Chemistry was evident when small talk led to the clasp of the hands, the old twinkle in the eye, and the former love which had been smothered in their parting several years earlier was rekindled within their hearts.

Because they felt they had wasted two years of their relationship they decided to plan for an early wedding in October in Manaus.

The couple arranged to meet in the Amazon's capital the following month to make their engagement official and set in order the necessary preparations for the wedding. After the wedding the new bride hoped to join Bill in Canutama, and so renovations had to be carried out on the old house to make it more presentable for the intended Mrs. Woods. For that reason James, a master carpenter and an ever ready worker, went down river with Bill to lend a helping hand.

They replaced the rotten timber from off the walls and floor and added an extension at the rear of the house to use as a kitchen. Bill not only enjoyed James' company and fellowship, but he greatly benefited from his expertise as a carpenter not to mention he was a welcome preacher at the meetings and a wise counsellor.

Late one afternoon while they were covering the roof of the new kitchen with aluminium Bill got a call to go to a house a little way down river where a young man had arrived from the River Mocuim. He had been bitten by a snake six days earlier. His brothers had carried him in a hammock in hope that the foreigner in Canutama — Bill, would be able to help them. James went with Bill, and when they got there they were horrified at the sight they saw and the foul stench of rotting flesh. The young eighteen year old was throwing himself about in the hammock while anxious parents were crying as they stood around. Some waved pieces of cardboard as fans to try to cool the boy's raging fever. Others tried to hold his gangrenous leg where the boy had been bitten several days earlier by the most feared snake of the jungle, the Surucucu or better known as the South America Bush Master.

Bill and James had little medical expertise, and they had nothing better than a few analgesics to offer the poor boy. After expressing their sympathy and admitting there was little they could do medically for their son, Bill offered to pray with the family. He told them, "We don't have any medicines, but I am a pastor and we are going to pray for you."

It was a harrowing experience for Bill and James, when even as Bill opened his mouth to pray the boy repeatedly yelled out in agony throughout the prayer, "I don't want you to pray — I want you to do something. I don't want you to pray — I want you to do something."

With a heavy heart and a feeling of deep inadequacy, James and Bill left that isolated house to return to town in the darkness. Even as they pushed the canoe out from the river bank they could still hear the boys voice echo in the still of the night, "I want you to do something."

This was not only a rebuke to Bill that there was little he could do, it was also a deep challenge, and even as they returned to the town he found himself saying, "Lord, help me do something for these people." Their visit to the distressed boy's house was on Friday. Early on Sunday morning the boy's brothers passed by the mission house carrying a hammock with the boy's corpse wrapped inside. The neighbours said they knew the boy had died when at 4 a.m. he stopped screaming, "I want you to do something."

The next morning in his devotions Bill still felt the rebuke of the previous evening and remembered not only the great spiritual need of humanity all around him but also the social and physical needs of these people. On his knees Bill surrendered his life again to the Lord and said he was willing to do whatever the Lord might have planned for him. He marked his Bible at a promise God gave him in response to his surrender, "The vision is yet for an appointed time, but at the end it shall speak, and not lie: though it tarry wait for it; because it will surely come, it will not tarry." (Habakkuk 2:3)

After the roof was put on the kitchen and the other renovations to the house were completed James offered to remain in Canutama while Bill went to Manaus to meet his intended wife and make necessary preparations for the coming wedding. However, there was a problem. The weekly airline service to Canutama had been disrupted for three weeks, and it seemed there was no way Bill was going to be able to be in Manaus for his engagement and to finalise plans for the wedding .

At the meal table it was customary to read The Daily Light, and on that morning the Lord gave a promise in the final part of the reading, "Now unto Him that is able to do exceeding abundantly above all that we ask or think, according to the power that worketh in us, ...be glory." James said, "Bill, I believe that is the Lord's Word and I feel the He is going to answer your prayers and today you will get transport to Manaus. Pack your case and be ready to go."

Both Bill and James knew that the Benjamin Constante, a large boat that travelled to Labrea and Boca do Acre in the rainy season, had been due to leave Labrea the previous night. Their expectation was that the Lord would cause the boat to call in at Canutama even though it was not in the habit of docking there. They were sure all things were possible with the Lord.

When the Benjamin Constante appeared around the bend of the river above Canutama, Bill was sitting at the river bank with his case ready to embark for the quick three day trip to Manaus. His hopes were sadly dashed when the boat passed by on the other side of the river, and the best they received was a wave of the hand from some passengers aboard.

Disappointed, Bill returned to the house with James and dared not ask about the promise the Lord had given them. The experience was discouraging but by no means unusual. On one occasion a pastor from the United States came down to Brazil to visit some missionaries from his church and spend several days with each. When he discovered he could only get a weekly flight into a place similar to Canutama, he was a bit frustrated but accepted the change in plans. A week in the small town surrounded by jungle seemed to be a long time to him, and he was glad when that week was finally over and he could resume his itinerary. On the given day he waited at the jungle airstrip for the arrival of the weekly flight. After three hours of evident delay he was quite exasperated, but that was nothing to how he felt when they got the news via the controller of the air strip, "The pilot forgot to go to your town this week but will do all possible to be there next week." Such was the relaxed pace of life in these interior towns.

Just as Bill and James scrambled together some lunch they suddenly heard the drone of an aircraft. They ran out and overhead they saw a Brazilian Air Force Catalina preparing to land on the river. Bill grabbed his still packed case and hurried to the river bank where he learned that news had arrived in Manaus of a revolt by wild Indians in the Canutama area, and several people had been killed. The

Governor of Amazonas had sent the plane to bring the bodies to
Manaus. It was a fictitious rumour for there had been no such
revolt. However, it did bring an empty plane to the town, and Bill
was offered a place on board, free of charge, for the return flight to
Manaus. The morning promise from The Daily Light had not been
in vain. The Almighty Lord had answered prayer in a most unim-
aginable way. Incidentally, Bill was not the source of the fictitious
rumour that led to sending the plane

In Manaus Bill and his girlfriend were kindly entertained by Mrs.
Denhem, an American missionary. For the young couple it was an
idyllic time of making preparations for the wedding, buying the rings,
meeting the pastor, sending out invitations and planning their future. The time passed all too quickly, and soon they returned to their
respective locations in the interior—Bill to Canutama and his sweetheart to the Boca do Acre. Their parting was tempered by the con-
solation that in just over two months they would be united as man
and wife.

Back in Canutama Bill made further renovations to the house,
and then wrote to his family and friends informing them of the
coming happy occasion. Mr. and Mrs. Cecil Harvey in Crossgar,
Northern Ireland received a prayer letter to be circulated to all Bill's
supporters and friends informing them of the glad news. Soon cards
of congratulations and best wishes were arriving for the blissful couple, and Bill was now counting the days when he would surrender
his single status. He corresponded with his loved one and told her
how much he was looking forward to the October date.

It was with unexpected shock and stunning sadness that Bill
received a letter from his fiance three weeks before the planned date
of the wedding to say that she could not proceed with the marriage.
Everything had to be cancelled. Being alone in Canutama was hard
enough, but this repeated heartbreak of all he had experienced
before while missioning in North Antrim but without the support of
friends and family was nearly more than he could bear. What should
he do? Should he quit the work and return to Britain? Should he
forget about all this mission work? These are the questions he wrestled with in his heart. They disturbed his sleep and dominated his

thoughts. Food was both tasteless and nauseating. Friends and colleagues were concerned for his safety. The Lord graciously placed people around Bill to help in this difficult time.

Painfully, Bill had to cancel the arrangements for the wedding; he also sent a hurried letter home to try to stop the circulation of the prayer letter with news of the previously impending wedding. Mr. and Mrs. Harvey had just got Bill's urgent and sad news as they were going out the door with the addressed envelopes ready for posting. They were shocked and frustrated, and they also had to scrap the letters. Their thoughts and prayers were very much with Bill.

Shortly after the cancellation of the wedding Bill's ex-fiance travelled to the United Kingdom on her first furlough. She never returned to Brazil. The whole episode was distressing and painful not only for Bill but for everyone involved. How often God takes our broken lives and shattered dreams, and with His unique skill as Creator, He makes something beautiful with them—in His time and in His way. It is sometimes hard for us to see that in order to gain what God has planned for our lives it might mean giving up what we desire. Of this Mr. A. W. Tozer prayed, "Lord I want to know Thee, but my cowardly heart fears to give up its toys. I cannot part with them without inward bleeding, and I do not try to hide from Thee the terror of the parting. I come trembling, but I do come. Please root from my heart all those things which I have cherished for so long and which have become a very part of my living self, so that thou mayest enter and dwell without a rival." Well might Bill have prayed Mr. Tozer's prayer.

Chapter Thirteen

No Never Alone

❖

The work at the church in Canutama and the demands on Bill's time continued in the lonely interior town. During the day he filled the hours with plenty of activity but the nights were long and often sleepless. His heart still ached from the recent trauma and he wondered when the hurt would ever go away. All the time the Lord was near and was silently planning in love for Bill.

One day he received unexpected visitors. Arne Abrahamson and Wilbur Pickering, two American missionaries, had paddled their small canoe into town. They arrived exhausted and hungry after weeks of surveying how best to access the unreached and remote Juma Indians on the nearby River Mocuim. After travelling for weeks they were glad to find a missionary living in Canutama and some ready hospitality. They asked permission to stay until a boat going to Manaus might come that way. Bill was glad to see them.

When they first arrived they were still sore from over exposure to the sun and from sitting in a cramped position for days on a small canoe. Both over six foot tall, they looked like giants in Canutama, and when they sat down to relax and stretched their legs out in front of them, their legs nearly filled the room. Once when Bill was going by where they were sitting he said casually and characteristically to Arne, "Get your big feet out of the way and let me by!"

Arne jumped to his feet and grabbed Bill, not to accost him as Bill at first thought, but he said, "Thank God to hear somebody normal!" Wilbur and Arne were good colleagues; Wilbur was a walking brain box and had five university degrees which affirmed his intellectual prowess. Both were family men who were fully committed to reaching the Indians for Jesus Christ. They had been pent-up on their tense river journey for weeks but had now found in Bill's home and company a place where they could be normal and relax. This was to be the beginning of a friendship between Bill and Arne that would open new avenues of service for Bill.

While Arne and Wilbur were with Bill Fred Orr and his companion Zezinho arrived by boat from Labrea, and almost immediately on their heels, Bill's good friend, Milton Rosa arrived by boat from Manaus. So much for being alone. The fellowship was good, and the conversations of various experiences and comparing notes seemed endless. At the church everyone enjoyed the variety of preachers.

In those days food was in short supply in Canutama. Seldom, other than on certain holidays during the year, was a cow ever killed for local consumption. The local populace depended on meat from the forest which was sometimes fresh deer meat or wild pig. On other occasions when even catfish from the river was not available, armadillo, tapir, monkey or even capybara, which is the largest rodent in the world, had to suffice. Thinking back on the occasion Bill does not know how they got through those days feeding six hungry men, but the experience helped Bill become domesticated.

Before the company left, Arne invited Bill to accompany him on a future trip up the Rivers Mocuim and Icua in pursuit of the Juma Indians. The visit of these friends and the full house had been a tonic of encouragement for Bill, and in meeting Arne, he felt he had entertained an angel unawares.

Arne returned a month later and brought supplies from Manaus for their expedition in search of contacts with the Juma Indians. The reports about these indians and their marauding attacks were legendary and struck fear in the local populace. Bill and Arne got a ride on the first part of the journey from Luiz Chagas whose medium size boat plied the River Mocuim selling goods and buying rubber and Brazil nuts.

After they travelled more than a day's journey up the River Mocuim they transferred their equipment into their canoe and headed still farther up river. It was tough work paddling the canoe in the hot sun and against the swift current. They tried to keep to the river's edge not only to avoid the main stream, but also to catch any shade available from the overhanging forest. The sound of the paddles cutting into the water did not frighten the surrounding wild life. Pink dolphins danced in the water. Alligators basked lazily on nearby sandbars ready to dart at any prey that might come near. Beautiful birds such as toucans, galca, mutum, macaws and parrots frequently flew overhead, and others such as kingfishers and bluetits seemed to accompany the progress of the canoe up river. Bill and Arne persevered paddling the canoe upstream.

By night fall they were ready to pull in at the river bank. Ignoring some of the hazards that lurked beneath the surface of the murky waters, they bathed in the river. After they were refreshed they prepared a meal from their supplies. After supper they lit a large camp fire to keep any unwanted wild life at a distance. They then tied their hammocks up between trees and enveloped them in mosquito nets. Dawn would come early so they settled down for the night and tried to sleep. Bill, usually a sound sleeper, woke in the night to the sound of twigs cracking as an animal lingered nearby. Without success he tried to waken Arne who was in a deep sleep. Bill pulled the sheet over his head and hoped the animal would not know the difference between his feet and his head. He lay still and tried to sleep again. Bill slept remarkably well. At daybreak the fresh paw marks discovered nearby were evidently left by a large jaguar and told the story of who the prowling visitor had been during the night.

After some black coffee it was then back to the canoe with all their equipment, and while the sun was still low in the sky they tediously paddled trying to make as much progress as possible up stream. From the Mocuim they entered into the more narrow and swifter flowing River Icua and persisted upstream. Finally they arrived quite fatigued at a rubber settlement called Santa Maria. To their surprise and Arne's delight a Juma woman and two of her sons and a daughter had come out of the tribe. The Indians had raided a nearby settlement, and in the counter attack many Indians were killed, and these four were separated from the rest of the warriors. In the skirmish, the fire of the surviving Indians of the raided settlement was lost, and without a perpetual flame they had no means of cooking food. Hungry and weak, the Indian family were obliged to seek the help of the Brazilians.

For Arne the contact was vital, but to their dismay they discovered that the men at the seringal had abused the Indian girl, and as a result she died a short while before the missionaries arrived. Arne soon realised no one could communicate verbally with the Indians so he stressed to Bill the importance of the language of love. "Show them that we are different," said Arne to Bill. "Love is the universal language," he insisted.

To try and comply Bill showed as much kindness as he could to Ited, the Indian mother, and the two small boys Petaba and Ica. They travelled for three days through the forest with the Indian family in the hope of finding the tribal village. On the expedition through the jungle the two Indian boys hunted and supplied small birds as fresh meat. The mother led on in what they believed to be the correct course through thick undergrowth to the Juma village. Bill got so exhausted with the trip he had to drop out. He decided to stay in an abandoned hut in a deserted village they had come across, but he insisted that the others continue in pursuit of their goal.

The party returned later only to find Bill fast asleep. Afterwards he thought what might have become of him if the Indians had attacked the others or if a prowling animal had stumbled on him. The Lord was merciful to them all. The search had been unsuccessful in locating the village so they headed back through thick jungle to Santa Maria.

When the small company arrived back at the clearing, the people who lived at Santa Maria were glad to see them, but they had bad news for them. Someone had stolen their canoe — now what?

Brazilians living in the forest are ever kind and willing to help out and so they offered the loan of a canoe to make the return trip to Canutama. Arne felt it would be wise to rest for a day or two before heading back down stream. He used the time to try to extract some Juma words from the two boys while Bill tried to major on the language of love, smiling and nodding at appropriate times.

One day just after his morning wash Bill was standing in front of a small mirror combing his hair when suddenly the Indian lady, Ited, lunged at him and caught him in her embrace trying to plant a kiss on his cheek. Bill had a struggle to finally push her away. Arne, seeing what was happening shouted at Bill, "Don't offend her!" When he had freed himself from his assailant he shouted back at Arne, "So much for the language of love, I think she is getting the message loud and clear."

The down river trip was not as demanding as paddling upstream had been, but six days to Canutama seemed to be a long way. Bill was glad when finally they broke out again to the River Purus and several bends up stream to the more familiar Canutama and home.

Several other trips with Arne followed to the same location during 1963, and on other occasions Bill showed hospitality to Arne and his wife Joyce when they passed through Canutama on the way to the tribe. The sad news came through that the younger Indian boy Ica had died from a snake bite.

The fame of Bill's hospitality must have spread, for soon others came to Canutama on the way to tribes in the neighbouring vicinity. Paul and Dorothy Moran were heading for a tribe on the River Cunhuáwhere Bill had travelled on his first trip with Jack Mawdsley. Paul Marstellar, the missionary pilot, landed his Cessna amphibian on the river at Canutama and had Bill store gasoline for him for the trips to the tribes in the area. Soon Canutama became a centre from which they were reaching out to the Apurina, Juma and Palmari Indians.

In all this Bill was greatly blessed, not only with the encouraging work of the church in town, but also in being a help to others in what he considered to be a more arduous task than his. One day he felt concerned about Arne being up river alone. Arne had been living near the tribe in hope of making friendly contact with the Indians. After prayer Bill felt prompted to send a letter to Arne asking to meet up with him at Jacinto on the River Mocuim on a particular date. The man who took the letter never delivered it. Unaware of this omission Bill travelled in the mission boat up to the seringal Jacinto on he pre-arranged date to see if there was any news of Arne's arrival. No one had any news for Bill. However, someone told him there was a boat due from up river that very day and maybe they would have some information. Bill decided to wait.

The waiting time expired and the trip seemed fruitless. It was time to return to Canutama. Just as they were about to leave someone called and said they could hear a boat coming. True enough within ten minutes a boat appeared round the top bend of the river upstream from the seringal. As the boat got nearer Bill could not believe his eyes. Arne was standing right out on the front of the boat.

When the boat got within earshot Arne beat Bill in asking, "What are you doing here?" Bill said he had come to see if there was any news of Arne. Arne explained that one of the woodsmen had fallen into a Juma trap and was injured. Besides, he had been feeling lonely and under pressure after six weeks in the jungle and felt he needed some fellowship in Canutama. The steps of good men are ordered by the Lord. Together they made the return trip to Canutama exchanging news of events in their different works and experiences in their lives.

Next morning in Canutama Arne awoke to a radio message from his wife Joyce telling him to come to Manaus urgently as their son had meningitis. God's timing was amazing. If Bill had not gone up river he would not have met Arne, and had Arne missed Bill, he would not have been able to get out of the tribe in time to be at the bedside of his boy.

The son fully recovered from his illness. The Abrahamson boys are now missionaries in Brazil and recall with great fondness the times Bill visited them either in their home in the jungle or when he travelled to Manaus. Bill's hilarious stories made him a favourite visitor who brightened their home and kept the children amused. Looking back on those days Dan Abrahamson recalls, "Bill Woods was a great colleague to my dad, and even though he seemed to face many difficulties he was always able to take things in his stride, and everyone was greatly helped by his jovial attitude to life. We appreciate him most because he was so willing to help mom and dad in whatever way he could although his own living conditions were meagre."

As a consequence of one of these trips in pursuit of the tribe Bill fell victim to hepatitis. The infection left him very low physically, and it was wisely suggested that he leave Canutama and go to Boca do Acre for rest. It was an enriching time of fellowship with James and Dorrie and Hazel Miskimmin who were all very supportive at this very difficult time.

From the Boca Bill went to Rio Branco for further rest. While there he visited the leprosarium six miles out of town. He was deeply touched and frustrated by what he saw — patients, plenty of them, many badly deformed and with a look of despair on their faces. There was little or no medicine available, and some young people were crying out with pain. The challenge Bill had felt in Canutama of trying to help these people filled his heart again, and he could not dismiss the despairing faces from his mind. He prayed that the Lord would enable him to be able to relieve the suffering of these people.

From Rio Branco he travelled over to Sena Madureira where Dona Zeli, a friend of James and Dorrie, looked after him for several weeks. The visit was refreshing, but Bill still felt physically spent and spiritually drained and requested permission from the home committee to return to Northern Ireland.

He was told to go to Manaus where money would be sent to reserve a place on the SS Hubert for the return sailing to the United Kingdom.

One final incident before Bill left Brazil was an indication of things to come. When he arrived in Manaus he stayed with Jack and Betty Finlay. Jack, from Belfast, had formerly worked with Acre Gospel Mission and married Betty, an American who worked with Baptist Mid-Missions. Jack was teaching at the Seminario Batista do Amazonas and introduced Bill to one of the students who was going through a particularly difficult time.

Miguel was a young man full of zeal for the Lord. He felt the call of God on his life and duly applied to the Baptist Seminary for study and preparation for the ministry. He was accepted and came to live in the dormitory at the rear of the college. He proved to be an excellent student and was making steady progress.

Miguel's studies were suddenly cut short just at the same time as Bill arrived in Manaus. Miguel had been suspicious about a discoloured patch on his skin and had gone to the doctor for treatment. Immediately the doctor diagnosed the tell-tale signs of leprosy. Miguel did not even have an opportunity to return to the seminary to pick up his belongings. Immediately he was whisked off to the leprosarium thirty kilometres out of town to be classified and put on treatment. Meeting Miguel was a milestone in shaping Bill's future.

Once aboard the ship to the United Kingdom Bill experienced an amusing and embarrassing incident. The passengers on the ship got to know each other very well after several weeks at sea. One morning while at breakfast with friends, Bill unavoidably sneezed, and the full force of the sneeze caught his bowl of Rice Krispies. When he opened his eyes, to his horror, he saw the lady across the table plucking Rice Krispies out of her lacquered hair. Apologies were made and accepted amid some fun at Bill's expense. When Bill sat at the same table the next morning amid the same company, he proceeded to open the Rice Krispies as on other mornings. He nearly fell off the chair with shock when the lady who had been the victim of his sneeze the previous morning asked her husband to bring her umbrella for protection against the threat of a re-occurrence of Bill scattering his cereal. The company and humour during the voyage to Britain greatly refreshed Bill and was as good as a tonic to him. The voyage also gave him time to wait silently in the presence of the Lord and to feel spiritually reinvigorated.

Photographic Section

ACRE
GOSPEL
MISSION

"ARDCARRON,"

SAINTFIELD ROAD,

BELFAST.

July, 1959.

Dear Prayer Partners,

Greetings in the precious name of our beloved Lord and Master.

It must be in a note of praise that I open my first prayer circular. The psalmist said, "The Lord hath done great things for us whereof we are glad." And I would echo his words of praise to the Almighty. Let me share with you some of the great things He hath done on my behalf. "O magnify the LORD with me and let us exalt HIS name together."

It was seven years ago this month when the Lord did the greatest thing of all for me—brought salvation to my darkened heart. "When free grace awoke me by light from on high; then legal fears shook me, I trembled to die. No refuge, no safety in self could I see. Jehovah-Tsidkenu my Saviour must be." It was on the 20th July, 1952, that I was CONVERTED; turned from idols to serve the living and the true God.

In years that followed I was often to be found in missionary meetings and conventions but never dreamt that the Lord one day would take me to the needy parts of the world. The first missionary I remember hearing in the early days of my conversion was Miss Mollie Harvey from Acre, strange that in years to come I was going to be CALLED to serve in that very part of the world! It was through a meeting at which Mrs. E. Eades, a missionary from the Cape Verde Islands, West Africa, was the speaker and later through the home call of Mrs. Ina Orr, en route for Boca do Acre, that I was challenged to dedicate my life wholly to Him.

Bill's first Prayer Letter

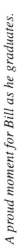

A proud moment for Bill as he graduates.

*'Ardcarron' the Old School House in Ballygowan where the Woods
family lived during World War II.*

*Bill in College uniform after his first term at Worldwide
Evangelization Crusade Missionary Training College.*

*George McClintock's milk float transporting Bill's baggage on his
first departure for Brazil.*

Bill as a new Missionary arriving in Labrea in September 1960.

Acre Gospel Mission Field Conference 1967.

Pastor Francisco Poderoso and Bill at the inauguration of the shoe workshop in 1970.

Dona Joanna, the lady who greeted Bill with a hug and called him 'an angel'.

Joao and Mario Nunes with son Ismael. As a boy Joao became Bill's first patient in Canutama when he discovered Joao's fingers stuck to a hot plate. Both Maria and Joao have artificial limbs.

No room for comfort on a canoe!

Stuck in the mud - again!

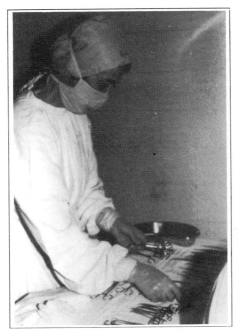

Nurse Emily Gilchrist preparing for surgery.

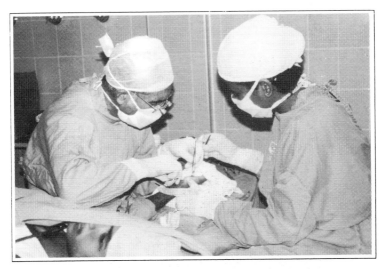

Bill operating on a hand with Dr. Cabral.

Bill's Acre Leprosy Programme Team in Rio Branco.

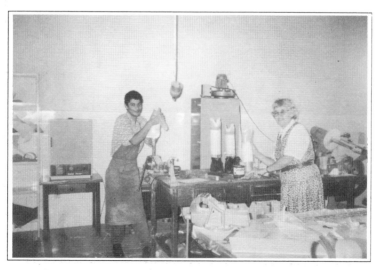

Nurse Ursula Milhan at work with artificial limbs in the Rio Branco workshop.

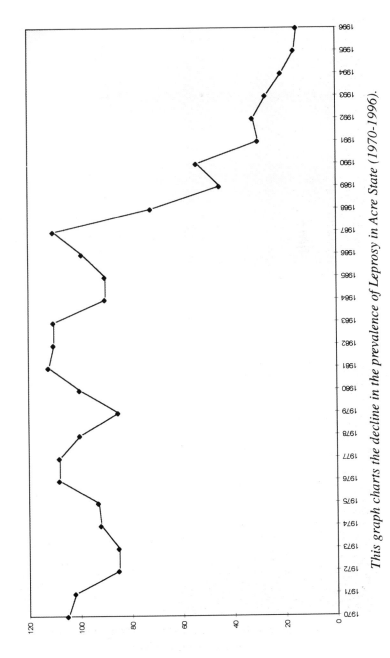

This graph charts the decline in the prevalence of Leprosy in Acre State (1970-1996).

Dr. Nordeen, Director of the Leprosy Dept. of the World Health Organisation, visits Bill's presentation of his work at the World Congress for Control of Leprosy, Florida, USA.

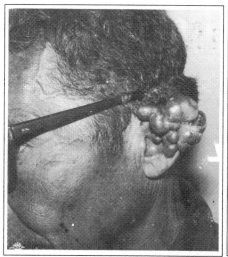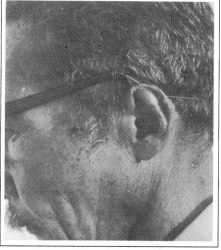

Bill also treats other skin disorders many of which are peculiar to the Amazon region of Brazil.

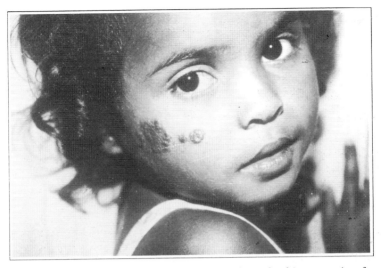

Chico Mendes who gained international fame for his campaign for the oppressed brought this young girl for treatment.
Before: Threatening deformity.

After: Free from the despair of deformity.

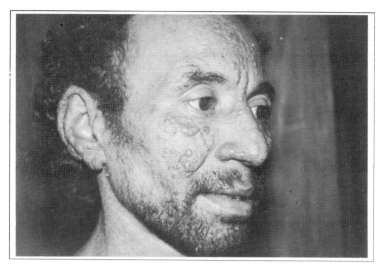

Before: Facial disfigurement from Leprosy.

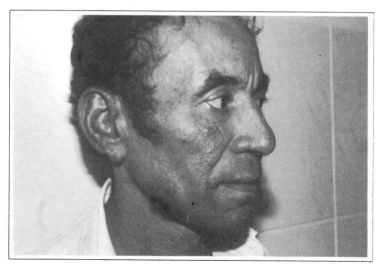

After: Face free from disfigurement.

Before: Sr. Milton became a recluse because of the scourge of Leprosy.

After: Sr. Milton is healed from his disease and free from despair.

Chapter Fourteen

First Furlough

❖

Bill's arrival home in Northern Ireland at the end of 1964 corresponded with the publication of the book Ten Fingers for God. Arne and Joyce Abrahamson had given Bill the book as a gift before he left Brazil. This book proved to be not only compelling reading, it was obviously something God had put in Bill's hands to shape and mold his whole future. The book tells the amazing story of Drs. Paul and Margaret Brand, missionaries at the Christian Medical College at Vellore in India, whose pioneer work of reconstructive surgery on leprosy patients brought relief to thousands on the subcontinent. The book had a profound effect on Bill's life. Paul Brand had been a carpenter before he studied medicine, but God tugged at his life constraining him to this avenue of service. Through dedication and determination he acquired skills that he used to the glory of God and to the blessing of many.

The testimony thrilled Bill, but it also challenged him to do something. Again he remembered the youth on the banks of the Purus who wailed in the night as death stole his young life, "I want you to

do something." Lord, I want to do something but what can I do?
pondered Bill. The answer seemed to come, "The vision is yet for
an appointed time... wait for it." Bill was to learn the lesson we all
find difficult to come to grips with—God is seldom in a hurry.

Bill's home church had kindly sent a generous gift to help in the
treatment of the young seminary student Miguel, and this was greatly
appreciated. But Bill knew that however worthwhile the donation
of money might be, it really was not the answer to many of the
needs he had left behind in the Amazon. He began to evaluate his
ministry in the light of his first term on the field. More time and
effort needed to be given to help, train and equip young Brazilian
men for the Master's work in their own land. The conviction that he
should also do something to help relieve some of the physical
suffering he had witnessed would not leave him.

Furlough for a missionary is often an intensely busy time, and
Bill was in constant demand to conduct meetings and speak at
missionary rallies all over Ulster and in Great Britain. He was able
to re-establish his close links with his friends in North Antrim
amongst whom he had ministered in earlier years. To all who showed
interest in his work he shared his burden for the physical as well as
the spiritual needs of the Brazilian people. He also told of the
promise the Lord had given him. Many people assured Bill they
would stand with him in his pursuit of doing the Lord's will. As the
months slipped by he decided it was time to take some decisive
steps to prepare for returning to Brazil.

At this time I (the author, Victor Maxwell) was studying in
London, and Bill contacted me to enquire from the renowned
leprologist, Dr. R. G. Cochrane, who had pioneered the use of dapsone
drugs that revolutionised the treatment of leprosy just after the turn
of the mid-century. Dr. Cochrane invited four of us to enroll in a
seminar for lay workers who might be interested in helping those
afflicted with this fearful and misunderstood disease. Susan Scott,
Audrey Smyth (three months later she would become my wife), Bill
and I attended the week-long seminar at Dr. Cochrane's Wimpole
Street clinic later that year. At the course Dr. Harman, also a former
missionary to India, gave us insights into the rudiments of the

various forms of the disease, its physical and social effects on its victims, and the diagnosis and treatment of the patients. It was a week well spent, but Bill still felt he needed to do more to help those he remembered near Canutama.

Bill then enrolled at the Missionary School of Medicine, near Holborn in London, for a three month course to cover the basics of anatomy, physiology, tropical medicine, dentistry and minor surgery. Unknown to him the three months at the Missionary School of Medicine were good preparation for bigger and better things that were to come. However, the course at the time was demanding and enlightening with attendants in many of London's hospitals and clinics. At the school he was also able to meet other students from different parts of the world and compare notes of what was happening there. Because of its proximity to London Bill had the bonus of being able to stay at Letchworth with his favourite Aunt Eve who had cared for him when he was a boy.

When the course finished in mid-December, 1964 Bill travelled home to Belfast for a few days to spend Christmas with his family. This proved to be the last Christmas he would have at home with the family for over twenty years and the last he would spend with his mother and father. It was also his last regular furlough for more than ten years. This period was broken with only a quick visit of a few weeks at the end of 1968. None of these things were envisaged by Bill at the time, but his Heavenly Father had planned other things for His child.

Those few weeks in Northern Ireland were a frenzy of hectic activity, seeing friends, conducting final meetings, packing and dispatching baggage, visiting family and taking the necessary injections and vaccines for returning to the tropics. So hectic was the schedule that on the day when Bill took his vaccine against typhoid he soon felt unwell. He went home and fell asleep and when he wakened he realised he had overslept and missed an engagement for a house prayer meeting where mission supporters met to pray for him and other missionaries.

His embarrassment was such that although still not feeling too well, on the next day he decided to call with the lady in whose house the meeting had been held. When the lady attended the ring of the doorbell she insisted that Bill come into the house. The room was warm and a large coal fire blazed up the chimney. He sat down and explained to the her the reason for the mishap and duly expressed his apologies. She was gracious and understanding.

Just then another lady member of the prayer group arrived for a visit, and in true Ulster fashion a cup of tea was served. For Bill, a combination of his own weakened state, plus the heat of the roaring fire and the non-stop conversation of the two ladies, was just too much. He is not sure for how long he slept, but he came out of a deep sleep with his head on a cushion and his arm slung over the arm of the chair on which he was sitting. The two ladies were still in deep conversation. If he had been embarrassed before he was now down right ashamed and beat a speedy retreat home in case another calamity should befall him. Not surprisingly, he was never invited back to that house meeting.

After some days at home for Christmas and the New Year Bill made his way down through England and across Europe to Hamburg, Germany, where on the 18th January, 1965 he embarked on a ship that sailed to the Amazon. It was a small cargo boat which could accommodated only three passengers—two Roman Catholic priests and Bill.

Chapter Fifteen

Back to Brazil

❖

H aving disembarked from the ship in Belem at the mouth of the Amazon Bill was held up for three weeks clearing his freight at customs after which he wasted no time organising his return to Canutama. There were however some things he wanted to see to in Manaus so he caught a flight to the Amazon capital. He wrote home at that time:

It was a great thrill to look down through the clouds and see once more the green carpet of the Brazilian forest stretching from horizon to horizon, to see the waters of the mighty Amazon River flowing down to the ocean like a great moving inland sea. I was now at last arriving in Manaus.

During my stay in the city I was able to make two visits to each of the Leprosarium Colonies. Each time we held meetings and visited the sick. On the first visit I went with a party of other missionaries. We hired a small jeep to take us along the muddy road through the forest. Going down a steep hill it was impossible to use the brakes because of the mud so the driver attempted to engage a lower gear, but once he put the jeep into neutral it was impossible to put her into any gear and before long we were completely out of control. Gathering speed the jeep skidded and bumped through the mud and deep craters on the "road". The Lord's hand was surely upon us.

My heart was once more greatly challenged by the awful need and conditions in these places. One young man, twenty-seven years old, told me he had been there for ten years, and although his family lived in the city, never once had they been to visit him in those ten years.

Bill went to visit Miguel who had responded well to the treatment he received in Sao Paulo and was able to resume his studies at the Baptist Seminary as an external student. Miguel also sported a new bicycle he had purchased with some of the donations sent out by the church in Northern Ireland. Bill further encouraged him to keep on his treatment and complete his studies. He graduated from seminary the following year and went to the Amazon town of Carauari where he pastored a Baptist church for almost thirty years. During most of those years Bill monitored his treatment, and today Miguel is completely clear of leprosy.

Bill gave first priority to help develop young men for the ministry in Brazil. Bill looked up his friends at the Regular Baptist Seminary of Amazonas and offered to take a student with him for one year to Canutama to gain experience in the work. Moacir Alencar had already completed two years study, and the course required the students to spend one year involved in a ministry, so he was chosen to go with Bill.

The river steamer Manauense took eight days to travel to Canutama. Again Bill was accompanied by Catholic priests. There were times and opportunities to witness to these priests, especially to Frei Vitorio who soon left the priesthood.

As the boat slowly made progress up stream Bill and Moacir took advantage of the ample time to get acquainted and to pray and plan a strategy for the coming year. Bill wanted to help those who were afflicted by leprosy and had no treatment. In order to do so Bill carried out a survey to find out who the patients were.

He planned to take Moacir on the rivers to evangelise those who lived in remote areas. Arne was already counting the days for Bill's return so he could accompany him on other expeditions to the Indians. His good friend Milton Rosa had died suddenly during Bill's year of furlough and was greatly missed in Canutama. Bill considered all these things and wondered what this new term held for him.

There were no missionaries in Canutama when they arrived, nor had there been any for some time. Jack and June Mawdsley had indicated they would not be returning to live in the town. Believers gathered at the boat for Bill's arrival and escorted him and Moacir the two hundred yards to the mission house.

Little could have prepared him for the shock he received when he arrived back in town. The mission house had been closed up for some time. Large rats ran freely throughout the property. For protection against the rodents, Bill's bed had to be elevated four feet off the floor. To acheive this height, he placed the bed on top of barrels. He was frightened to even imagine what would happen if he inadvertently put his foot out of bed in the middle of the night and plunged four feet to ground.

Bill soon tired removed the bed from the top of the metal drums, tucked his trouser legs down his socks to prevent the rats trying to find an escape route up his leg. He unpacked the small air gun he had brought from home and there followed what seemed like a shootout at the OK Corral.

Now that he was back in town other people began planning Bill's future. The mayor came to him and explained that the local educational system was desperate. The local teachers could take the children no further than the fourth grade of primary education. He wanted Bill to teach fifth grade and allow some bright young people the opportunity to continue their education. Bill was unable to refuse the request, and some of these students turned out to be the brightest young people in the church. Because of those classes there emerged the founding of the "Escola Rui Barbosa," the first Christian school in Canutama which at first was housed in an old dwelling at the side of the church. It later developed into a much larger school with uniformed pupils and four Christian teachers

Dona Conceitao brought her ten year old grandson to Bill and explained that her daughter who lived up river, didn't have the where-withal to rear Martins. "Could he come to study with 'Professor Guilherme' and live in with him and Moacir?" Martins was a sturdy little boy who wanted to study and was willing to work. Bill again could not refuse this request so Martins was given a room at the back of the house in which to hang his hammock.

Bill did not need to look far for leprosy patients in his town. Fourteen year old Joao who lived immediately across the street star-tled Bill one day when he brought a plate of very hot food to the door. The plate was too hot for Bill to hold so he went to find a cloth to protect his own hand. When he tried to pick up the plate it would not release from the boy's hands so Bill tugged at it. He found that some of the flesh from the boy's fingers had fused to the underside of the extremely hot plate, and the fingers were bleeding with second degree burns and many blisters. Because of leprosy young Joao had no feeling in his fingers and as a consequence didn't know his hands were being burned. Looking up at Bill with his outstretched bleeding and blistered hands he said, "It's all right. I don't feel anything."

Sr. Bispo on the down-river side of town lived in seclusion because he was afraid to go out with inflamed skin patches over his body. Sr. Xavier lived in abject poverty nearby. He had suffered rom leprosy for many years without any treatment. His fingers were gone and his feet were barely stumps at the end of his ulcerated legs. Another Joao lived in degrading destitution in an old fallen down shack still farther down river. He was a sad sight to behold. Joao Batista was the son of the leading deacon in the church, and it was a traumatic experience when he was diagnosed as having leprosy. But these were not the only cases, and the list continued to grow as new leprosy sufferers were discovered almost daily.

In November of 1965 Bill wrote home from Canutama:

Last week I was asked to arrange some medicine for a boy who had dysentery. I gave some medicine to his father. Later I was passing the house and decided I would call in and have a look at the boy. They told me I could not see him as he was indisposed.

I thought that was strange and sat down and told them I would wait. After some time when they saw I wasn't going, they took me into the back room where I met the boy. It is true he was very ill with dysentery, but he was also suffering from an advanced case of leprosy. There were lumps, patches and infections all over his body. His fingers were all gone, his legs and feet were deformed. He had virtually lost the use of his legs and could not move very quickly. I don't know how long he had been suffering from dysentery. He was lying on an old bed—the mattress and the floor were in an incredible mess. The family were burning breu (tar) in the room to kill the foul smell.

I wasn't long getting them organised. They soon threw out the old mattress and had the room washed and disinfected. He is now taking a bath every day. I have him on vitamin injections to build him up before starting him on the treatment for leprosy. I also forbade the rest of the family to use the room. I had often been to that house but never knew they had a boy hidden in the back room. He is only sixteen years old. His cousin also suffered severely from leprosy. However, after dozens of injections and the Ciba 1906 drug he is now able to do his work in the centre where he lives.

These are only a few of the patients Bill registered for treatment with Dapsone—the only drug recommended and available at that time. Bill not only administered and supervised the treatment. but where necessary, he bathed and dressed the wounds. The results brought relief to the patients and were most encouraging for Bill. Again he wrote home about that time:

Altogether I now have twenty patients on treatment for leprosy. Those who live right here in town obviously have an advantage. Some of these have to take daily injections to relieve the pain in the infected nerves. It is encouraging to see the progress they are making. My mornings here in town are entirely taken up attending to them and to so many others who come with everything from malaria to cuts and burns.

The patients who live on the rivers are desperate for help. Recently we travelled on the River Purus at night by aid of a full moon. One evening we pulled into a place at about 8:00 p.m.. While there we heard there was a man who had leprosy. However, we also learned he had been abandoned by his family and had gone to live near a lake. I got a young man who knew the way to accompany me. We set off by canoe and when the moon disappeared we used a kerosene Tilly Lamp to show the way. The journey took two hours each way, but it was worth it just to see the man and give him some hope as we put him on treatment.

After the patients in town had been given their treatments, Bill with Moacir, old Joao and Martins set off on a month's river journey down the Purus into the River Tapu and up the remote River Cunhu. Every day they stopped to evangelise the forest dwellers, treat the sick, register leprosy patients and give them some initial treatment for their disease. Although the meetings were encouraging, Bill was frustrated by meeting leprosy patients who he knew would remain in their remote isolation which would make regular, supervised treatment impossible. It weighed heavily on his heart.

Again Bill travelled on the River Mucuim. He gave an account of the typical hardships encountered on some of these trips:

The boat I travelled on was packed with Brazilians going up to the various centres in the forest to cut rubber during the dry season. There were about twenty-five aboard although the boat was little bigger than our own that generally sleeps four. Added to this. we were sitting on top of bags of mandioc and sugar or salt as the men were taking their supplies with them.

During the day the heat was terrific, and at night the cold was just as bad. I tried to get a few hours sleep curled up in a canoe that was tied alongside the boat. Besides me there were three other men wedged in at various parts of the canoe. Talk about living close to the people—it was a bit too close for my liking. I had a towel rolled up for a pillow and wondered how it was getting wet. Just then someone suddenly shouted "We are sinking!" The canoe had flooded. It didn't sink, but we got wet, and if the cold was bad before, it was even worse afterwards. Due to the heat during the day I felt like a wet blanket, and at night because of the cold and damp I was wrapped up in one.

In November, 1965 Audrey and I (the author, Victor Maxwell) joined Bill in Canutama after language study in Labrea. The year and several months that followed held times filled with incident and blessing. There was growth in the church and the school. Whole families came to the Saviour and the Young People's Fellowship developed greatly. Together we worked at finishing the church building and then employed our forces to construct a school building at the rear of the church.

The only source of stone near to Canutama was a day's journey up the River Mucuim where we worked under water to break stone on the river bed. Once the canoe was filled, we headed back to town either to sell the stone to raise funds for the school or to put it into the foundations of the building. This exercise was repeated many times until we had manually broken under water and transported more than twenty tons of stone.

Besides this, Bill and I combined some of the things we had learned at the Missionary School of Medicine to help the local populace. Bill's responsibility was to classify and treat those who fell foul of the ever present malaria as well as to care for the leprosy patients. I did most of the dentistry and offered to help in any emergencies that arose out of the frequent fights, the deadly snake bites and the regular accidents in the town. There was no other medical help for hundreds of miles, so the little done by these two amateurs was greatly appreciated even if at times it was hit and miss.

On one memorable occasion I engaged in a bit of emergency dentistry. A man had arrived with excruciating pain in a lower molar. I took him into the little clinic room we had at the side of the house and duly applied the local anaesthetic in the region of the tooth. I then rocked the dental forceps as we had been taught and struggled to removed the decayed but obstinate tooth. My heart sank when I heard a crack and the upper part of the molar crunched into small pieces leaving the root still deeply embedded. Try as we did the root refused to budge. I gave up and offered the man a few analgesics. I told him to come back the next day in the hope the root would have loosened.

I wasn't at home the next day when the man called, but Bill came to the rescue to help relieve the man's pain. He remembered that for a situation like this some crushed codeine and a little oil of cloves was helpful on the offending tooth. The problem was Bill wasn't sure how much a "small drop" of oil of cloves was. For good measure Bill stirred a spoonful of the oil and mixed it with the crushed tablet and emptied the lot on the broken tooth. It really should only have been one or two drops of the oil on a cotton bud. Even as he poured the mixture into the open mouth the poor man leaped from the chair in agony and ran into the street. The oil of cloves had roasted his mouth. For he next half hour the poor man ran up and down Canutama main street until the burning subsided. Thankfully he did not seek revenge. After that incident we felt we should hang a plaque outside our house warning, "Danger, Saints at Work!"

Our arrival in Canutama took some of the responsibility off Bill and left him free to travel more on the river and devote extra time to what he felt the Lord was laying on his heart. Paul and Dorothy Moran, another couple from Wycliffe Bible Translators came to Canutama on the single engine Cessna plane, and after a few days Bill took them on the long journey to the River Cunhuá to leave them with the Palmari Indians. As they travelled Bill was able to visit the leprosy patients he had contacted several months earlier as well as evangelise at the river settlements.

Arne was a regular visitor during that year in transit either to or from the Juma tribe. The progress of his work was painstakingly slow. During Bill's absence Arne had been trying to encourage friendly contact with the tribe. On his visits to the jungle he left fishing hooks, cotton and nylon lines and plastic buckets which Bill had given him for the Indians. These buckets angered the Indians and almost cost Arne his life. When the Indians filled the buckets with water and tried to boil the water on the fire they discovered the fire burned the bottom out of the buckets before the water even heated. The irate Indians blamed Arne for fooling them.

After some prayer and careful planning, Bill and Arne decided that they would make an attempt to go into the tribal village and take with them the Indian woman and her remaining son as translators and hopefully mediators to speak to the Indians. Arne's wife, Joyce, and their sons planned to travel with them. Armed with supplies for a month and under-girded with much prayer they left Canutama for the two day journey to Sao Francisco on the Icua where the Abrahamsons had built their rustic jungle home. It was an exciting but also an apprehensive time.

After unpacking at the centre on the River Icua, they spent some days gathering together a group of trusted men who would go with them on the planned trip. Bill had brought with him a reel-to-reel tape recorder and a tape series of studies from the Epistle of Paul to the Romans conducted by Pastor Willie Mullen of Lurgan Baptist Church. Each night before retiring they listened to one of the studies which proved both enlightening and encouraging. On the night before the planned departure for the tribe there was obvious anxiety, but no one dared mention it.

Bill and Arne sat down to listen to the next in the pastor's studies which should have been in Romans chapter 8. To their mutual bewilderment Pastor Mullen announced his text as 1 Samuel 23:16, "And Jonathan, Saul's son arose, and went to David into the wood, and Jonathan strengthened his hand in God. And said unto him, Fear not." The pastor majored on the last words, "Fear not." He pointing out that these two words are repeated 366 times in the Scriptures—a "Fear not" for every day of the year plus one for Leap Year. The message seemed to be tailor made exactly to suit Bill and Arne on the eve of their trip to the Indian village.

Later when Bill enquired from Pastor Mullen about the message and the friend who gave the tape, neither could explain why that sermon should ever have come up in the middle of a series on Romans. God's timing was exact for them, and the words were appropriate to calm any anxious fears. That night both missionaries strengthened their hand in God, in His promises, in His protection and in His presence with them. Both men felt humbled to know that the Lord had brought this message just for them. The time of prayer that followed seemed like the gate of heaven to them both.

Bill wrote the following of the trip:

At 7:00 a.m. on Friday 14th January, I set off with Arne Abrahamson along the trail through the jungle leading to the Indian villages. We were about to make another attempt to contact the hostile Juma Indians. Exactly three months before, Arne had met an Indian lady along the trail, and she went off screaming. He was soon surrounded by six men. They took everything Arne had and left him with only the clothes he stood in. That was the first contact with this unreached tribe.

What he didn't know and was to learn later is that several pairs of eyes were observing him. Arne also discovered later that an arrow had been trained on him, but a wave of the Tuxau's (the Indian Chief) hand spared the American missionary.

The tall trees gave ample shade from the sun which got hotter as the day went on but did not spare them from the draining humidity which caused them to perspire profusely. Persistently they swung machetes as they cut their way through dense, lush undergrowth. Sometimes they were down on their hands and knees to creep under the heavy brush. Petaba knew of some hanging vines that gave refreshing drinks of clear cool fluid, and these were greatly appreciated.

The difficult hike through the jungle took them up steep inclines and then plunged them down into muddy swamps. They crossed streams and small, dangerous rivers; sometimes they waded or swam through the water; at other times they edged gingerly across on fallen trees. Bill remembered that in the forest there was an abundance of snakes, and in the rive—alligators, sting ray fish and piranha. They also kept a vigilant eye for the feared surucucu snake or a hungry jaguar.

Petaba hunted and caught some wild monkeys for the evening meal. In the evening they lit a camp fire and cooked the meat which was eaten with toasted manioc. After hammocks were swung between trees and the fire fuelled to burn well into the night, a time of prayer reassured their hearts that their lives were in the hands of their Heavenly Father. Encouraged by the prayer time but totally exhausted from the tiresome trek, Bill slumped into the hammock. Not surprisingly, he fell asleep almost immediately.

They were all awake before dawn at 5:00 a.m., and after some cream crackers and a brew of strong Brazilian coffee they moved on through the forest—at times through heavy rain. By 5:00 p.m. they had reached the first Indian village. It was burnt to the ground but was still smouldering. There were obvious marks and signs that the

Indians had left on the trees. Petaba said the signs meant death awaited anyone who went on. He was manifestly frightened, and the atmosphere grew tense.

Arne was concerned for all who were with him on what he felt was the mission God had given to him."Why risk the lives of others to accomplish what God sent me to do?" he reasoned. He suggested that Bill turn back.

To this Bill replied, "What about the message on Pastor Mullen's tape and the promise God gave us? Didn't He say 'Fear not?'"

It was discovered later that the Indians were watching and waiting for them to turn so that they could shoot arrows into their backs. The fact that they went on surprised the Indians. If it had not been for Pastor Mullen's sermon, they would have turned back and fallen into the Indians' trap.

Later Bill reported about the entry into the village:

Just outside the Indian village there was the design of a man carved on a tree and plastered with red dye — not a very welcoming sight. A little way ahead of us was a fresh trap set across the pathway. An unsuspecting person might have fallen into the hole and onto the spears that were pointed upwards. We could hear the Indians talking. The Brazilian woodsman and the Indian boy were terrified. We waited for about half an hour to see if any of the Indians would come out to the trail to meet us rather than us walk into the open area between the edge of the forest and their village. Our wait was in vain.

Because it was getting dark we returned along the trail where we spent the night in an old shelter belonging to the Indians. It was nothing more than a palm leaf roof over our heads, and we slept on the ground. Our clothes were wet and because of the heavy rain earlier that day we could not get a decent fire going.

It was bitterly cold during the long hours of the night. Eventually the dawn came, and with it the first rays of sunlight began to trickle through the dark forest. As we moved off we wondered what the day held for us. The last people to meet these Indians were a man and his wife. They were found sometime later — he with three spears through his body. The Indians had severed the wife's head and taken it off with them. Prior to this another man had been found with five Juma spears buried in his chest and his eyes pulled from their sockets. The Lord said, "Go to every creature... and lo I am with you always." He was certainly with us that day.

We got to their village about 5:30 a.m. and moved slowly among the tall corn stalks until, through the green, we spied the semi-circular palm leaf covered communal house used by the Jumas. It reminded me of a big circus tent. Inside the large house each family has its own fire around which they sleep. Slowly and carefully we moved into the house. The embers of a fire were still warm indicating that some family had been there, but now no one was at home. The atmosphere was tense with apprehension and expectation. Arne had Petaba called out friendly greetings in the Juma tongue, but no answer came. Hidden and quiet the Indians watched from a distance. The woodsmen and Petaba were terrified. The latter had reason to be afraid. The Indians had already speared his mother to death and had also tried to drown him.

We went outside again and hid among the tall corn stalks and waited for the Indians to return. At one stage we thought we could hear them, but they did not appear. After waiting a long time there was a rustle in the corn, and when we looked, there nearby, was a large jaguar picking its way past us. When it saw us it took off in haste.

We returned again to the Indian's house and waited some more. Taking advantage of the dry interior of the house I lay down and soon fell fast asleep on the mud floor. I had a rude awakening when two Indians walked in — a man and wife. We spent about an hour with them trying to convince them we were their friends and giving them presents. The man tried hard to get my shirt and my shoes off, but I tried harder to keep them on — I won. Among the presents we took them was a cooking pot, but the woman was not too pleased for she thought it was too small. Trust a woman even in a remote place like this. They told us that when the new moon would be up, the other Indians would all be in this village and to come back then. I found their clothes interesting — they didn't have any! Praise God for the peaceful contact.

After several hours with the couple the party left with a lighter heart and were relieved and grateful that they had not only made contact, but had also been preserved from danger. On the following day the group arrived back to the houses at the edge of the river. The missionaries hoped the Indians might even venture out to the clearing near to the houses. On occasions the Juma had raided some of the neighbouring rubber settlements and "stolen" equipment and food. To our mentality it was stolen, but they left behind bows and arrows and feather head-dresses obviously in "exchange" for what they had taken.

Bill had to leave and return to Canutama. Arne stayed on and hoped to go in again a week later in another attempt to make friends with the Juma. Petaba and his mother Ited went with Arne and the forest men on that trip. Again they were disappointed and decided to return but Ited left the group and decided she was going back to live with her own Juma people. Sadly the next time she was seen there were eight Indian spears plunged into her body. She had been seen with the "white men" and this was the sentence they meted out on her. For Arne it was a chilling reminder of how dangerous his mission was.

After Bill left Canutama for Boca do Acre, he received a letter from Arne dated 24th October 1967, in which he related further contacts with the Jumas:

Once again, I can say from experience that prayer moves the hand of God. Your prayers took us, kept us and brought us back from the Juma Indians. After our return to Brazil, word reached us that the Indians were waiting at Iyaya for us. With great expectancy on July 27, Stanley, my fourteen year son and I arrived in Canutama. Immediately I began to seek information from the Brazilians concerning the Indians. I was told that their last appearance was on June 16. On that date they came to Sr. Elclete's house. He was not there as he had gone fishing downstream. The Indians took everything that was in his house. This new information was quite a blow for me, but His ways are not our ways. We must not lean on our own understanding but commit all our ways unto Him. He is a powerful and precious Saviour, and happy are they who put their trust in Him.

When we arrived in Iyaya there was no one there. Sr. Antonio's family and Sr. Elclete had moved to the opposite bank of the river. They were now living about five minutes upstream so we spent the night with them.

The next morning, Stanley, Pidaba and I went to live at Iyaya. Since we were going to be staying there, the Brazilians decided to come down during the day to make farinha.

The second day, Sr. Elclete, Antonio, Chico Tomaz, Jose-the son of Elclete, Mirte his daughter and Chico's wife and three children all came to make farinha. After a meal of boiled turtle, meat and farinha, the two boys and I were resting in our hammocks in our house. The farinha house was very nearby — about three quarters of a block away. All of a sudden all bedlam broke loose. The Brazilians were screaming and hollering that the Indians had arrived.

I grabbed some necklaces and ran toward the confusion I could see the young chief was trying to take the baby away from Chico's wife. Other warriors were roughing up the men. After I yelled, all the Indians came running toward us with their bows and arrows. When they saw the necklaces in my hand, they began to calm down. I motioned to them to follow us back to our house where more presents were given.

Some of the Indians lay down in our hammocks. When they finished lying down the hammocks were tinted red from the dye that rubbed off their bodies. I could see from their facial expression that they were intent on taking our hammocks. I got them all to go with me over to where the Brazilian men were still working. The women and children had fled in their canoes. While we were gone Stanley and Pidaba took our hammocks to the Brazilian's house across the river.

The night before the Indians had killed a tapir so they wanted to take some farinha with them to eat with the tapir. Wild reeds were gathered in order to make large baskets to carry the farinha in. The young chief told Pitaba they were expecting us to carry the baskets back to their village. I told Pitaba to tell him we would not. I knew once we started that they would always expect it. The end result would make life almost unbearable for the Brazilians. No more was said concerning the baskets.

The next morning the Brazilian men were going to go back to make more farinha. I told them not to go, for the Indians would be expecting them to carry the baskets of farinha. If they refused the Indians would become very angry. However, against my advice, they went anyway.

When they got there the Indians grabbed two men and tied baskets to their backs. Joseé was thrown to the ground, and they began to pluck out his eye brows. The two men with the baskets refused to move. This infuriated the Indians so much so that they were at the point of killing the men. At the last minute the Indians took the baskets and went off into the jungle. Prayer truly moves the hand of God.

We waited several days for the Jumas to come back, but they did not return.

A short time after this Arne Abrahamson made other friendly contacts with the Indians and quickly gained their confidence. He and Joyce eventually went to live in their village and over a ten year period invested much time learning the language and reducing it to writing and then translating the Scriptures. Sadly the Jumas engaged in what was virtually self-destruction. Many of their people had been killed in raids, others were victim of "foreign diseases" such as colds and chicken pox. Then they began to kill each other.

After his mother died Petaba lived with the missionary couple for several years, but sadly he also died in his early teens, a victim of what we call "the common cold." The remains of the tribe now live as friendly neighbours among the forest people on the River Icua. Arne and Joyce continue to work in Rondonia, Brazil. After more than thirty-five years of sacrificial service, they still have contact with the surviving Jumas. Four of the Abrahamson's six children returned to Brazil as missionaries.

Chapter Sixteen

God Speaks Again

❖

Just after breakfast one morning in Canutama a lady came to our door in great distress. She asked that we go to a nearby house where a boy had just arrived from up river and was dying of snake bite. I grabbed a little first aid bag, and with Bill we went to visit the house almost despairing of anything we might be able to do. Fifty yards from the house we smelled the stench of rotting flesh. We took a deep breath and went into the dark wooden hovel. All the windows were closed and the air reeked with a foul smell. A mother and father sat weeping at the side of a hammock in which their ten year old boy Francisco, lay staring up at the palm covering above. His body was partly covered with an old piece of cloth. The mother pleaded with us to do something for her boy.

When they pulled the cloth back the sight that met our eyes made both of us recoil. Just below the knee of the right leg the rotten and gangrenous flesh was separated from the bone as if it were old bark falling from a decayed tree.

I asked how long Francisco had been like that. They related an all too familiar story. Francisco was getting ready to go fishing with his father. Between his jungle home and the canoe he was bitten by the deadly South American Bush Master snake. In the isolation of the jungle they had no medicines, and terrified by superstition they immediately hid him from "the evil eye" lest someone should look at him and put a death spell on the boy. Far from any medical attention the extremely poor family applied the hardened yoke of a boiled egg and leaves from the jungle to the wound in a vain attempt to have the venom drawn out of the boy's body. This continued for ten days by which time the area surrounding the snake bite had already started to decay.

The boy continued to burn with fever so the family decided to seek help elsewhere. They prepared their dug-out canoe and laid him on an improvised stretcher sheltered by banana leaves. Rowing from dawn to dusk it took them six days before they finally arrived at Canutama, and they called us almost as soon as they arrived.

As feared, there was little we could do for the suffering boy. We washed the wound as best we could, wrapped the leg in layers of cotton wool doused with loads of talcum powder to counteract the awful smell and made him as comfortable as possible. We prayed with the family and asked the Lord for a miracle to help the boy. It was a matter of "before they call I will answer and while they are yet speaking I will perform." Just as we were praying a Catalina plane flew low overhead preparing to land on the river. It was Thursday, the day of the weekly commercial flight from Manaus. Haste was important, for if the boy missed this flight, another week would be too late for him to escape death. Bill and I hurried to the river's edge and got a canoe out to the plane to speak with the pilot. Having listened to the plight of the suffering boy he readily offered to give him and his father free transport on the return three-hour flight to Manaus.

Miraculously Francisco survived surgery that very day when he had his leg amputated near to the groin. After recovery and a short time of physio-therapy and re-habilitation, he and his Dad returned to Canutama and from there to the seringal. Life in the interior jungle is difficult for an able bodied man, but a for a young lad with one leg the prospects were grim. Bill saw the dilemma of the family and offered to provide an education for Francisco.

Bill takes up the story

Two years slipped by. I had now left the work in Canutama in order to take up medical studies in the city of Manaus. Francisco was in my care, for his parents had no means of educating him. It was my intention to one day take Francisco to one of the large Brazilian cities in the south of the country in search of a mechanical leg.

An initial test in Manaus gave me a terrible shock. The doctors told me that the muscles of Francisco's stump were already wasting and a mechanical leg would be useless unless it was fitted immediately. What was I to do? I had no financial means to be able to fund passages to the south. I remembered the saying, "Only he who attempts the ridiculous can achieve the impossible." Was this a ridiculous dream I had planned for Francisco?

In vain I tried to arrange free flights with the Brazilian Air Force. I was told, "Next year—perhaps." Even then, next year would be too late. Somehow the story of Francisco became known to the Governor of Amazonas, Dr. Danilo Mattos Aerosa, and immediately he offered to provide our flights to Rio de Janeiro on a commercial airline.

As we approached the beautiful city of Rio I realised that the friends with whom we would be staying lived high up in the hills that surround the city. That meant we needed a taxi which would cost us $10, and we were on a very limited budget. However, a gentleman on the aircraft began to ask some questions about Francisco and where I was taking him. The man was a captain in the Brazilian Navy and offered to help in any way possible. It was enough to know he lived in the same area in which we were planning to stay so he took us right to our host's door. That saved the expense of a taxi.

The next morning Francisco and I stood outside the Red Cross Hospital. The president of the hospital read the letter I had brought from the Governor of Amazonas appealing for help for Francisco. He apologised and explained there was nothing the Red Cross could do.

Outside the hospital I looked at the constant flow of traffic on the busy street and wondered what I was going to do with this boy so far from home, and I had very little money. Just then someone called me back into the Red Cross Hospital building and suggested I try the Children's Corner in the hospital's grounds. I soon discovered that this "Children's Corner" was a place where, besides serving hot chocolate to the poor street children of Rio, all sorts of problems were solved and help given to scores of people.

Dona Zulma was the kind-hearted lady in charge, and after hearing our story, she soon had us in the hospital ambulance on our way to the Ministry of Health's office. She introduced us to the Secretary of Health for Rio who received us with the greatest courtesy and attention. He informed us there was a special grant for children like Francisco, but it would only be available the following year. That was of no use to us.

Next morning we visited the offices of the "Globo," Rio's largest daily newspaper. A young reporter listened to our story, and after taking some notes he hugged Francisco and said, "Don't worry my son. We'll get you a leg."

Meanwhile, Dona Zulma rang the Secretary of Health and told him Francisco's story was to be published in the "Globo" and would be telling of his failure to help the boy. Within a short while we had a call from the Secretary to say a special fund had been released and the leg could be fitted immediately.

Before the week was out Francisco was walking without his crutches and proudly swinging his new "leg."

This episode with Francisco gave Bill further incentive and stimulus toward the goal he felt the Lord had put on his heart — to equip himself to help relieve much of the suffering in this region. He shared with us how he felt. His commitment to the leprosy programme was heavy on his heart, and now he was convinced the Lord wanted him to study medicine.

The University of Amazonas had only recently developed a medical faculty. Previously medical students had to study in Brasilia or the south of Brazil. To Bill this opportunity to study so close to home was further confirmation that he should follow this course. Even though the demands of teaching in school, preaching in the church and travelling on the river left little time for anything else, yet Bill disciplined himself to study physics, chemistry, biology,

Brazilian history and geography in the discomfort and oppressive heat of Canutama without so much as a fan to help him cool off. Often he literally burned the oil lamp late at night and into the wee hours of the morning. He knew he would need his educational transcript, so he sent home for the records of his junior and senior certificates of higher education. This was the beginning of a road that would take Bill a long way from those quiet and obscure beginnings in the old house in Canutama.

Just after Christmas 1966 there was great excitement when the river steamer Tavares Bastos pulled in to Canutama. Fred Orr and Robin McCready had come to Canutama for a visit, and they joined Bill, Audrey and me when we boarded the large vessel. Already on the boat were Hazel Miskimmin and James and Dorrie Gunning returning from furlough, Lenore Graham, Thelma Peters and Dr. Tom and Ethel Geddis—all new missionaries recently arrived in Brazil. There followed six days filled with good fun and fellowship as the boat steadily made its way up-river to Boca do Acre. We were all bound for the annual Field Conference. The injection of four new recruits for the work was the sort of spiritual tonic we all needed.

At the Boca do Acre Mollie Harvey and Susan Scott had made great preparations to receive the missionary party. When I recall those days and how scarce and meagre the supplies in the interior towns of the Amazon were, I think Mollie must have had a heart like a lion to receive and entertain such a large "family."

For the next week we met in conference with daily devotional sessions, and then we got down to the business of assessing the work and designating workers to where they were needed most. In the shake-up of that conference Bill was invited to go to work in Boca do Acre and replace James and Dorrie Gunning who were going to Sena Madureira while Hazel Miskimmin would join us in Canutama.

This move was most timely and obviously designed by a Higher Hand and planned by a Loving Heart. Shortly after Bill arrived in the Boca do Acre he had a few pleasant surprises. Francisco Poderoso, who was only a boy when Bill first visited the Boca in 1960, was now student at the Regular Baptist Seminary of Amazonas in Manaus and had returned to his home town to do his field term for a year and work alongside Bill. The friendship forged between these two had not only made a great impact on the evangelical work in the town but also would develop to open the horizons into the treatment for leprosy patients far beyond the bounds of Boca do Acre.

Also, the town had recently received a new doctor from the south of Brazil. Dr. Eduardo was not a Christian but was impressed with Bill's interest in helping the needy patients in the town, and almost immediately he struck up a rapport with Bill and Francisco. The three rented an apartment above a chemist shop in the middle of town. Francisco and Eduardo took advantage of having an English teacher present with them and greatly developed their language skills. Bill in exchange used Eduardo's medical knowledge to help with his preparatory studies of physics, chemistry and biology.

Another token of the Heavenly Father's providential care was evident not long after Bill arrived in Boca do Acre. During the transfer from Canutama to Boca do Acre Bill travelled seven days on the steamer Almirante Alexandrinho. It was an unpleasant trip, and Bill had repeated spells of fever and vomiting which he blamed on the food served on the boat. Once he arrived in the Boca do Acre his condition seemed to improve and he thought little more about the sickness.

Several weeks later he suddenly took another bout of vomiting. He was glad there was a doctor in the house and on examination Dr. Eduardo diagnosed appendicitis. Had this happened a few months earlier in Canutama with no medical help available and little hope of an emergency exit from the town, it could have been a lot more sinister.

Later writing of his experience Bill recounted:

Recently I have been thinking of some of the places I have visited during the past year. There were the trips to Juma Indian villages which took three days by boat and then two hard days walking through the jungle; there was the isolated homes on the River Cunhua which entailed seventeen days of constant travel in the Mensageiro da Paz; still further there was the home of the backslidden Christian who needed to be visited by the missionary taking an eight hour walk through the forest, at times wading through flooded jungle chest deep and at other times swimming across the river.

It was in none of these places I became ill, not even in Canutama, where there is no doctor, but right here in Boca do Acre where the local doctor lived in our house and was able to prescribe some drugs while we waited three days for the first available flight to Rio Branco. Again, conscious of God's leading and provision for in Rio Branco I was able to have Dr. Tom Geddis perform the operation and then immediately afterwards was taken to their home where I received the best possible attention from Tom's wife, Ethel.

After the conference earlier that year Tom and Ethel Geddis had gone to Rio Branco for their language study. Mollie Harvey's earlier friendship with the state governor's family had reaped benefits for Tom and Ethel who by courtesy of the governor were given accommodation in an apartment at the new Maternity Hospital. Bill, suffering from acute appendicitis, unexpectedly arrived on Tom's doorstep, and after another medical consultation he was interned for immediate surgery—in the Maternity Hospital.

Dr. Tom, assisted by Dr. Silvestre, another surgeon friend, operated on Bill that very night and removed his appendix. As Bill came round from the anaesthetic Tom jested to him, "It's a boy! What will we call him?"

Bill, although still dazed and groggy from the anaesthetic, yet with characteristic wit and humour whispered, "Paisley!" referring to his own minister and renowned controversial political figure in Northern Ireland.

"What will we give him to drink?" Tom further teased.

"Orange juice, of course!" answered Bill.

The programme of meetings and commitments in Boca do Acre was excessive. Apart from the church in town there were weekly meetings across the river in Sao Paulo where a small Christian school also operated. At Terra Firme, where Susan Scott lived, there was another church and then other meetings in various preaching points up river, down river and out through the forest. It was necessary that Bill be fully recovered from his operation to be able to cope with this heavy load.

As Bill regained his strength he took on an even heavier work load. He and Francisco made it their business to register the leprosy patients in and around Boca do Acre. Not only did they discover numerous patients who immediately were started on supervised treatment, but many of them had ulcerated wounds. Dr. Eduardo's help was solicited for other medicines and kindly granted to help them in this work. Bill and Francisco made regular visits to these homes to bathe the wounds and apply dressings where necessary.

One of these patients was Dona Elsa who lived at Monte Verde, over an hour's journey from the Boca. She recalls, "I remember the Saturday morning when Sr. Guilhereme came to our humble home. Others were afraid to come near our house. He not only came in but examined the large ulcer I had just above my ankle. He also examined the rest of the family, but I was found to be the only one with the disease. He gave me tablets and promised to come every Saturday morning to bathe and dress my ulcer. Thanks to him and Pastor Francisco my wounds began to heal."

Trips were also made out into the surrounding forest both to evangelise and to treat needy patients. Francisco remembers, "We walked for hours and then had to wade almost neck deep across streams to get to some of those places. I was a lot younger than Guilhereme but found it hard to keep up with him. He seemed untiring in his endeavour to reach still more people and do more work." On one of these trips Dr. Eduardo also accompanied them on a vaccination campaign. One trip was enough for him. He was unable to walk for days afterwards.

In a letter to Mr. McComb in 1967 Bill stated:

This week has been a little fuller than usual, for heavy rains have postponed a meeting in the home of one of the believers. On Thursday afternoon I go to visit a leprosy patient in Monte Verde; it is a good hour's walk from Terra Firme. On Fridays I go to Senhor Raimundo for the meeting there. Last time we went it took us eight hours to do the journey, but I hope that this time it will take less. The trail is rather muddy, in fact, I understand at one point it is necessary to swim.

Next week I go to another centre for a meeting. This second trip is the longer. I went there last January, and the brother was away from the Lord. Since our visit he is bright for the Lord and in the work so it is worth it to visit these distant places and encourage those who live there.

Pedro Morais today is the pastor of the Evangelical Baptist Church in Boca do Acre and he recalls, "Francisco and Guilhereme made a big impression on my life the year they were here. I was so challenged by their dedication that at the end of the year I surrendered my life to the Saviour and left home to go and study at Bible School." In 1997, Pedro marked his twenty-first anniversary as pastor of the church in his home town.

While the spiritual and medical work in Boca do Acre was both demanding and rewarding, Bill felt the Lord was telling him to take a further step and go to Manaus and prepare for the entrance exams at the University of Amazonas. This was not an easy step and at times was misunderstood by friends and colleagues. However God was calling.

Writing letters is a major part of a missionary's life and often is his life-line. The letter Bill wrote from Boca do Acre to James Gunning, the field leader in Sena Madureira, at the end of 1967, informing him of his plans to leave the Boca and remain in Manaus after the Field Conference, was both crucial to Bill's future and far-reaching in its implications. It was not only a difficult letter to write, but once written Bill needed the reassurance he had done the right thing.

While the letter was still in Bill's hands he was weighing up in his mind whether or not he should send it. Just then Fausta, the sister of one of the leprosy patients across the river, came to the door and said to Bill, "Mother wants you to know that Sebastiana can't go back to school because the ulcer on her foot is getting bigger." Sebastiana and her brother Milton were two severe cases Bill and Francisco had been treating.

"Does she want medicines?" Bill asked.

"No. She just wanted you to know," the girl replied. The girl's answer hit Bill like a bolt. "Was it the mother who wanted me to know, or was this God letting me know?" Bill pondered. Prompted by this unexpected visit from the girl and the message from her mother he sent the letter without any more hesitation.

Later that same day after he had despatched the letter to James, Bill received correspondence from friends at home. On opening the mail a quotation at the head of the first page caught Bill's eye immediately, "Where God's finger points — there God's hand will make the way." His heart was reassured he had taken the right step.

Pedro Morais, Francisco Poderoso and Bill travelled to Manaus together, Pedro to start at Regular Baptist Seminary, Francisco to complete his final year and Bill to take the next step.

Chapter Seventeen

Manaus

❖

January 1968 was a special time for many of us in Acre Gospel Mission. In the recently acquired mission apartment we had our annual Field Conference at which Audrey and I were asked to go to Boca do Acre and fill the big gap left by Bill's exit. Immediately after the conference two of our missionaries, Robin McCready and Thelma Peters, were designated to work Canutama. Four days after the wedding our first daughter was born in Manaus at the Policlinica.

Bill Woods took up residence in the Amazonian capital, and there he stayed for the next seven years. Arne and Joyce Abrahamson kindly opened their home to Bill until he found somewhere to live. Dona Lygia Rocha, a very keen believer and well known language teacher, made available a small apartment to rent at the rear of her house. There was also room to accommodate Francisco Poderoso during his final year at the seminary and then subsequently when he accepted the call to be pastor at Berea Regular Baptist Church. This remained Francisco's home until he got married to Cirene a few years later.

Bill's chief purpose for being in Manaus was to devote his time to study in readiness for the entrance exams to university and the medical course. Within weeks of his arrival in the city the exams started. Although Bill had revalidated his senior certificate from home, he still had to study physiology, physics and chemistry. At Belfast High School the teacher had advised Bill to drop physics before his junior certificate exam, and Bill gladly complied.

He met with a group of other students who were also hoping to gain entrance to the university's medical program. Each person in the group was an expert of sorts in one of the fields of study so each helped the others. The studying continued until 2:00 and 3.00 a.m most times. When they finished at that unearthly hour all the fellows hailed taxis to take them home. Bill was too embarrassed to offer to go with them for he had no money to pay his share of the fare. He diplomatically found a reason to remain until after they all left, and then he walked the two miles home.

When they sat the final entrance exams all of the group gained admittance except for Bill. He might have been tempted to ask why this should be. Bill felt he had applied himself to the studies as best he could, and now he had to commend the future into the hands of his Heavenly Father and trust Him. If the Lord were in all these developments, then He would lead on and help him clear another hurdle.

He remembered he had already refused the option of going to university in Northern Ireland at the end of his formal education. Now to make it to university in another country and in a foreign language would not be easy. It just so happened that for the forty places available in the medical program, only thirty-two people had passed the first attempt at the entrance exam. Bill had been eliminated in the first attempt because he failed in the physics paper, a subject he had wrestled with before.

Another exam was convened for the remaining eight places. One hundred fifty people entered that exam. Bill gained second place in the results and was overjoyed when he saw his name published on the list of those who scored sufficient credits to gain entrance to the medical course. Surely this was the Lord's doing.

Bill's success in obtaining entrance to the university proved to be the climax of a very eventful year. However, in order to pursue the university course Bill was obliged by the mission committee in Northern Ireland to take a leave of absence from the Acre Gospel Mission. This development made survival in Manaus very difficult for Bill as his monthly allowance terminated with the leave of absence. Things became even more complicated because friends at home were not made aware that Bill had ceased to receive his monthly support from the mission. Envisaging an uphill programme of study with insufficient funds ahead, Bill decided to take a short break in Northern Ireland to visit his family.

As ever, calamity seems to stalk Bill in his travels, and this trip was no exception. En route to the UK he took Manoel, another young man from Canutama who had had his leg amputed, to Rio de Janeiro to be fitted with a new artificial leg. When he was due to embark on the flight to Europe he emptied his pockets of all his Brazilian currency and gave it to Manoel. He embarked for the overnight trip to Europe. First they went to Lisbon where he stayed a few hours to make a connection. From there he went to Zurich where there was yet another delay while he waited for an on-going flight to London. By this time, not having had opportunity to wash or shave, his stubble had grown for almost thirty hours and made him feel sticky and untidy. At the Zurich airport he noticed an electric razor for general use in exchange for a coin. Bill found a few cents in his pocket and exchanged them for local currency. He put them into the machine and began to take the beard off. Halfway through the process the electric razor ceased to function. Time was up, and Bill had no more coins for the machine. He was a little embarrassed to arrive home with one side of his face clean shaven and the other with almost two days growth.

He shared with the mission committee and his home church and friends what the Lord had done for him and outlined the path ahead as he saw it. He had decided to defer the beginning of his medical studies until early 1969 and in the intervening year concentrate on establishing a viable base for the work he felt he should be doing amongst leprosy patients. Although he was on leave of absence from the mission, he was assured that personal gifts would be forwarded to him and the support of his own home church would continue. Encouraged by the prayers and support of many, Bill returned to life in Brazil. He didn't know it would be the last time he would see his father and mother.

Manaus had just recently been granted the status of being a zona franca — a tax free zone, which permitted many foreign and multi-national companies to set up business and industrial plants in the city to supply the Latin American market. This was most propitious for Bill. To supplement his support he began to translate and teach English at private classes. He was not averse to following the example of Paul who occasionally reverted to tent making so not to be chargeable to anyone.

The late Milton Rosa, who was a frequent visitor to Canutama where he had given the mission a house, had been a great friend to Bill, and this friendship continued with his family after Milton's sudden death. Milton's son, Valdir Rosa, who had been to England with Jack and Joan Mawdsley and spoke very good English, made the most lucrative contacts for translation, and these provided ample work for Bill. With the money gained, both Bill and Valdir invested in buying sites and constructing houses for quick resale. This was done several times over and not only helped keep body and soul together over a few lean years but was used to finance several projects in the leprosy programme.

Invitations constantly came for Bill to preach in the growing churches of Manaus. While he was able to accept many of these invitations, he had to limit himself to attendance at Faith Regular Baptist Church where he not only taught Sunday School but became the church pianist. As well as his secular employment and church activities, Bill's help was solicited by many people who had formerly lived in Canutama and Boca do Acre. Some of these had fallen on hard times either financially or physically and were without the wherewithal to pay for medicines or treatment. It was hard to refuse people in need, so Bill found himself ministering to the social needs and demands of many families.

Francisco Poderoso accompanied Bill one day to a seminar at the leprosarium in the colony of Antonio Aleixo. Several American nurses and para-medics from the National Hansen's Disease Centre at Carville, Louisiana, in United States, were demonstrating newly developed shoes with Plastisole lining as an insole which gave protection and care to the mutilated and deformed feet of leprosy patients. This insole distributed the pressure of the foot to relieve the most vulnerable pressure points which often were the sites of the most gruesome ulcers. So many of the patients Bill and Francisco had treated suffered from large plantar ulcers on their feet. These ulcers were largely caused by lack of sensation and consequent injuries to the foot brought about from stepping on thorns, glass or nails. Because of the lack of feeling they didn't suffer pain from the ulcer, and with diminished circulation to the tissues the ulcers only got worse. A custom made shoe for each individual patient offered greater protection for the damaged feet.

Convinced that this was a project they could and should venture into, Bill procured funds from the sale of the house he was building to send Francisco to Dr. Paul Brand and friends in Carville in the United States to learn the technique of making orthopaedic shoes. In the meantime they needed premises for consultations and the necessary machinery to make the shoes. The Lord provided a place in a marvellous way. The Cachoeirinha Regular Baptist Church near to Bill's apartment offered them a piece of land at the side of the church on which was erected a small edifice that provided a consulting room and a workshop.

While Francisco was gone Bill had been put in touch with Mr. George Macedo from Rio de Janeiro through the contacts at Carville. George Macedo was the Brazilian National director of CERPHA—Commissao Evangelica para Reabilitatao de Pacientes Hansenianos, an organisation Bill had helped found. George also represented the interests of several leprosy organisations in Brazil including the American Leprosy Mission. He was excited about what Bill and Francisco were trying to do in Amazonia and made some funds available to help secure some of the equipment needed. However, most of the funds came from gifts that people in Northern Ireland had donated for Bill's support.

Bill started his medical studies in March 1969 and at that time met friends at the Hospital Alfredo da Matta, a dermatology centre in Manaus where many leprosy patients were treated. They supplied Bill with the names of their most needy patients. Bill visited many of these and outlined to them the plans for the clinic. A slide presentation was prepared to educate people about leprosy and the benefits of these preventative measures.

When Francisco Poderoso returned from Carville, he immediately went to work with Bill to make the workshop function. The front part of the small building was a waiting room with educational posters on the walls encouraging the patients about the advantages of the treatment. Gospel leaflets were also available, and Bible texts were posted on the walls. Next to the waiting room was a small consultation area where the patients' feet were washed in disinfectant. Bill then examined the feet and an impression was taken of each foot on the heated Plastisole mold. Once the impression was made Francisco then went to work making the leather upper for the boot or shoe. An appointment was made for the patient to return for fitting and periodic inspection.

The results were dramatic. People who had been confined to their homes and not able to walk because of chronicly ulcerated feet saw their feet heal very quickly, and soon they were able to walk and often return to places of employment. One example was Sr. Benigno. When he arrived his plantar ulcer was so bad it was possible to put a pencil up under the sole and it would appear on the upper side of his foot. This wound was treated every day, and very soon the fissure closed, and his foot healed due to the treatment.

Another patient had a fish bone embedded in the foot ulcer without his knowledge of its presence. The bone was discovered, removed, the foot treated, shoes supplied and again the result was astounding.

Every week Francisco made at least a dozen pairs of shoes while Bill supervised the treatment of the patients. He also encouraged physio-therapy on the atrophied legs, arms and hands. This work was slow and time consuming, but it was also very rewarding just to see the transformation, both physical and social on the lives of the patients. Better still, the workshop was a place where some patients were converted to Jesus Christ.

On 16th January, 1971 the Manaus daily newspaper, "The Critica," published a photograph of Francisco at work making shoes with a short report:

In a small but efficient workshop at the Cachoeirinha Baptist Church, this craftsman makes special shoes for patients suffering from leprosy: Sr. Francisco Poderoso, an evangelical pastor, who obtained his special training in the United States. We recently carried a report of his work in this paper. These special shoes, shaped in the steel molds to provide the maximum protection for the patient, are greatly welcomed by all leprosy sufferers at Antonio Aleixo Leprosarium. None of them now need to risk injury by walking on their bare feet.

By the time the clinic was fully operational Bill had already started his studies at university. Francisco continued to pastor the Berea Baptist Church on the opposite side of Manaus, and it was an extremely busy period for both of them. At that time Antonio Farias, a Christian medical student at the university moved into the apartment thus helping with the general expenses and providing another student to accompany Bill with his medical studies.

As the studies picked up momentum Bill with his friends Primo Faneli, Wilki Baia, Udo Medeiros and several other students formed a study group. It was a regular habit to rest a little in the early part of the evening, and then, when the oppressive heat of Manaus diminished somewhat, they would meet at 10:00 p.m. and study through until 4.00 a.m. Bill dosed himself with Coca-Cola and coffee to help stay awake. Next morning they were back at the university for classes at 7:30 a.m. or off to their place of employment. With this study programme plus the workshop and other eventualities, there was no room for social activities.

When the news of Bill's father's death came through it emphasised that another family link had gone. Bill longed to go home to comfort his family, but the demands of study, the low budget and the distance from home made regular visits to Northern Ireland impossible.

Chapter Eighteen

A Tough Course

--- ❖ ---

Bill's first year at university had been extremely taxing on his time and energies, and the small workshop for leprosy patients proved to be nearly too much for him. Just at that time Bill was alarmed to feel pain in the calf of his legs. He consulted Dr. Wallace in Manaus, a well known physician and surgeon who had cared for many of the missionaries. Concluding his diagnosis Dr. Wallace broke the news to Bill and shocked him, "I am concerned for your condition and think you could have leprosy. I would like you to have other examinations."

Bill felt the best place for these examinations was at the National Hansen's Disease Centre in Carville, Louisiana, United States, where he had already established contacts with Drs. Paul and Margaret Brand. When he arrived Bill was immediately interned in the leprosy unit and classified with his number as a leprosy patient. But thankfully, after careful examination, it was discovered he did not in fact have the disease but was suffering from a combination of malnutrition and physical exhaustion — a result of the heavy pressure of his activities whereby he was over worked and under fed.

The experience initially shook Bill. Having assured so many that leprosy was one of the least contagious of communicable diseases, he, at that stage, thought he had fallen victim to the bacteria. After his fears were allayed he realised one reason he possibly had been allowed to experience the terrible trauma of being registered as a leprosy patient. The Lord had graciously permitted this to happen to him so he would have an understanding what it was really like to be diagnosed as being stricken with leprosy. The turmoil and uncertainty of those weeks gave him greater empathy with the patients than he ever could have had if he had not passed through that experience. Today Bill can sit down and say to his newly diagnosed leprosy patient, "I have been there."

Back in Brazil George Macedo was so impressed by the great success of Bill's first workshop in Brazil making these specially designed shoes that he asked Bill and Francisco to go to Belem, the capital of Para, to set up a similar programme at the Marituba Leprosy Hospital. For one month they gave lessons to the staff appointed to this work, and within a short time the Marituba workshop was producing seventy pairs of shoes per week for the many patients they served all over a vast area of northern Brazil.

Following the success of the workshop in Belem, again through George Macedo, Francisco and Bill were invited by the Ministry of Health in Sao Paulo to conduct a training seminar for a workshop at the Bauru Leprosy Hospital which is four hours drive from Brazil's largest city. Both Bill and Francisco relished the hospitality given them when a limousine was sent to pick them up in Sao Paulo and drive them to the to the hospital.

Bill set up other shoe workshops in the southern city of Curitiba and in Campo Grande, one of Brazil's strategic interior cities. The course in Sao Paulo became the spring board from which those trained at Bauru Hospital went to other state capitals to teach the same techniques for making orthopaedic shoes to those involved in leprosy programmes. Within a short while thousands of patients all over Brazil were benefiting from the project pioneered by Bill and Francisco in Manaus several years earlier.

Today in Rio Branco the programme has come full circle. In the Acre, Ursula Milla, a German missionary nurse who attended the shoe workshop course supervised by those trained by Bill in Sao Paulo, now operates a first class workshop that not only makes shoes, boots and sandals, but also artificial limbs for many patients and supervises their physio-therapy to make the limbs functional.

With the wider national programme of workshops for limbs and shoes in operation, the need for the programme in Manaus diminished over a period of time. The Manaus workshop/clinic functioned for seven years, right through until Bill graduated from university. Scores of people were literally put back on their feet, and today they lead useful active lives in their communities. The redundant equipment was donated to the other programmes in Manaus, Sao Paulo and Belem, and the premises returned to the friends at the Cachoeirinha Baptist Church.

After the workshop closed the talented Pastor Francisco Poderoso was offered lucrative positions in the social and medical fields in Manaus and even in Africa but felt he had a higher calling as pastor of his Baptist Church and a commitment to training others pastors in Amazonia. He went on to become the national president of the Association of Regular Baptists Churches of Brazil, the director of the Regular Baptist Seminary of Amazonas, a Gospel singer with several recordings and all this while still remaining at his church for almost thirty years. He gives credit to much of what he learned in Christian devotion balanced with practical living to the years he spent working with Bill Woods both in Boca do Acre and Manaus.

Francisco related:

Bill's life challenged me to trust God for everything. Often in those early days in Manaus we were not sure where the next meal was coming from, but we prayed, and in miraculous ways God never let us go hungry. The Lord did not give us a menu to choose from, but with what He sent, sometimes it was just a hand of bananas, we learned to be content and thank Him for His gracious provision.

The days in Boca do Acre taught me the value of each individual, one life, one soul and every one was precious to God. This was the vision Bill imparted to me, and I am glad it has remained with me all these years.

Besides this, I benefited from his encouragement when I was a young pastor and faced problems I had never met before. Added to all the devotion, study and work, we had many a good hearty laugh, and Bill's sense of humour was super. He had the fine quality of being able to laugh at himself and make others laugh also at some of the calamities he told us of. It was his obvious modesty that made him speak of his own blunders and give us all a chuckle at his expense.

Dr. Antonio Farias, who also shared the apartment with Bill and Francisco until he left to be married, is today a well known medical practitioner in Manaus. He heads up the Evangelical Clinic which has an extensive ministry to the Christian community and to many needy cases who are without any financial resources to fund their treatment. Recalling those days of study he remembers how Bill was a great example to them as Christian medical students:

He was ever conscientious to the point of being a perfectionist. What he considered to be a low mark in an exam was a high one for us. What amazed us was his work rate. During the day he was supervising the shoe workshop with Poderoso, overseeing the building of a house near the cemetery, giving English classes during the week, preaching the Gospel at the weekend and studying late at night, and yet he was scoring higher than most of us.

With all this work he never let the pressure of the study get to him. One day he arrived home and told us he was bringing a woman home to live in the apartment. Francisco and I stared in amazement at each other and wondered what we were going to do. Had Bill found a woman at last? He then told us that he had been to the cemetery and bought a female skeleton from the cemetery's groundsman. It was supposedly to help with his study of the skeletal system in the anatomy classes. Ever a master of being inventive Bill dipped the bones in lime to make them white and then pieced them together with wire. In assembling the skeletal frame Bill found this nameless creation had two right legs and no left leg. When he had the full stature of the woman he decided to dress her up. We fitted her out with a long sleeve blouse, a skirt, gloves, shoes, a scarf on her head, false teeth in her mouth and a pair of dark glasses to complete the model. We sat her in a rocking chair and had our photos taken with our "pin up". Bill claimed her as his own and called her "Maria". Great fun was had at Maria's expense.

The next day Bill was in the shower when Dona Lygia Rocha, the landlady, called at the door. When there was no reply she quietly opened the door only to be confronted with Maria in the rocking chair! Her frightened yell nearly brought Maria to life. Dona Lygia thought she had stumbled on a real life experience of Hitchcock's film Psycho! We had a job convincing her of our motives.

I asked Bill one day why he had come from so far and wanted to study medicine in Brazil. He told me he wanted to specialise in ophthalmic surgery to enable him to give sight back to leprosy patients who suffered blindness as a result of their disease. That was the measure of the man. He was always thinking of others even to the point of at times neglecting himself.

This point made by Dr. Antonio was also greatly borne out by Antonio Sampaio Nunes whose family came from Canutama:

When my parents lived in Canutama back in the mid-sixties, we had nothing. One sister had already died, and the other had to be sent to Manaus seriously ill. Bill Woods paid for the flight for her as my family couldn't afford it. Because of my sister's illness my Dad sold his canoe and the few chickens he had and took Mum and us to live in Manaus. Like most migrant families we fell on hard times. Money was difficult, but my father got a job as caretaker of the Second Baptist Church in Manaus.

When Bill came to live in the city he was often invited to preach at the church so he kept in touch with Mum and Dad. By this time we had started school but with little or no money Dad could not afford to buy the required reading or exercise books for us. Periodically Bill slipped him money to help buy these or provided him with paper and pencils to help with our education. This kind gesture continued until he left Manaus to study elsewhere.

We never saw him again until fifteen years later. One day my father called me to go with him to someone special. From one of my book stores in the centre of Manaus my Dad had spied Bill Woods getting into a car which was taking him to Antonio Aleixo. We drove thirty kilometres out of town to Antonio Aleixo where Bill was consulting at the clinic.

When we met him he was shocked and pleased to see my Dad. There was a lot of back slapping and hugs. With tears in his eyes my father introduced me, "Antonio, you owe your education to this man. When we had nothing he gave us money to help buy pencils and books for you and your brothers." That night all our family took Bill out for a meal. He has remained a good friend of our family, and we feel that all we have we owe to him."

Sitting in the comfortable surrounds of his plush air-conditioned office from where he manages his three educational bookstores in downtown Manaus, Antonio continues his story:

It was only later we found out that Bill Woods didn't have very much money himself in those days. I discovered that often he had to walk to the university because he had inadequate funds to afford transport, and yet, out of his little he sacrificed to give to my family. We could never repay him for what he did. For us he is a real man of God.

As the training course at university developed from the classroom to practical work in clinics, Bill continued to make contact with other leprosy patients at Alfredo da Matta Clinic and the Leprosy Hospital at Colonia Antonio Aleixo. The head nurse at the clinic, Maria del Pilar Rodrigues says:

Dr. Bill has always been a very willing worker with our programme here in Manaus. I have known him since 1971, and we have been impressed with his dedication to the patients and with his professionalism in his work in Cruzeiro do Sul, Rio Branco and Manaus. Initially his work with the Alfredo da Matta Clinic was caring for those who had ghastly plantar ulcers. After he graduated and qualified as an ophthalmic surgeon he has been unstinting in giving time and employing his skills in ophthalmic surgeries at Aleixo and here. Many patients who had limited vision or impaired movement of the eyelid now enjoy better use of their eyes. Dr. Bill is a dedicated doctor and yet a very humble man who is held in the highest esteem by all at Alfredo da Matta.

It is hard to believe that with a loaded study course at university, clinics and hospitals to attend and the supervision of the workshop at Cachoeirinha, Bill was also actively involved in Christian work.

During the last year before Bill's graduation Francisco Poderoso married Cirene and moved out of the apartment. Antonio also tied the matrimonial knot and left. Bill resisted any move to follow the example set by his flat-mates. However, he decided to vacate the apartment and go to live with the pastor's family at the rear of the Faith Regular Baptist Church in the Santa Luzia district of Manaus.

The Faith Church had a very well organised soul-winning programme. Teams went out to different parts of the city to reach beyond their immediate community to some of the outcasts of society. Besides being pianist at the church Bill linked up with one of these teams. One night a team brought to the church a young delinquent they had met on the street. Vicente, who originally came from Tarauaca, was an intelligent and well-educated young man but his tangled life was in a grim mess. Drink and drugs had virtually left him as a down-and-out on the streets of Manaus. His life was ruined, his marriage broken, his job gone. He was in the depths of despair with the bottle and the needle providing his only solutions. He hung around with a gang of underworld thieves and drug peddlers, sleeping rough in derelict buildings or wherever he could lay his head.

"You know my life," Vicente Gurgel told the Sunday morning congregation at the Second Baptist Church in Manaus where he is now an associate pastor. "I was down in the gutter. My life was ruined by drink and drugs and all the immoral things that accompany these evils. God sent an angel, His messenger Bill Woods, to tell me of a better way in Jesus Christ. God used His servant to take me out of the quagmire of sin and corruption and miraculously turned my life around."

The transformation in Vicente's life was not immediate. After the initial experience of conversion he was soon back on the bottle and back to his old haunts. He remembers that on those too frequent occasions when he became a prodigal and again went down that road to ruin, Bill went after him. At times Bill found him in the houses of ill repute where armed gangsters and bandits hid out. It was not uncommon in these hideouts for men to be knifed or given an overdose of dirty drugs. He tried to warn Bill not to go into such dens of iniquity, for Bill's life would be in danger. Notwithstanding the danger, Bill persisted in trying to rehabilitate Vicente. Even when his family had given up hope and wanted to wash their hands of him, Bill still endeavoured to rescue Vicente's life.

Today Vicente has completed seventeen years in pastoral work, and he confesses that he owes his life to the perseverance and zeal of God's servant. "He was not only used to rescue and rehabilitate me, but he encouraged me to study the Scriptures and engage in evangelistic activity. In wonderful ways God opened doors for me to serve Him, and I learned so much from Bill who was my mentor."

It was a great day when Bill graduated from medical school. The long years of hard work and conscientious study reaped dividends when he topped the graduation class of 1974. When his name was called to receive his diploma, all the students stood to cheer him in recognition of his great achievement. He would have loved his mother to have been present for the graduation night when they placed the diploma in his hand. He was now Dr. William John Woods MD.

Chapter Nineteen

Rio and Eventually Home

❖

To achieve his medical diploma in a foreign language was no mean feat. A good rest and holiday would have been more than justified and was perhaps needed. But it was not for Bill to lie back on the laurels of his success nor in his nature to take things easier. On the very day after graduation he left Manaus for Rio de Janeiro to start two years of study at the Miguel Couto General Training Hospital where he specialised in ophthalmic surgery.

Because his arrival in Rio corresponded with the end of the school year he was able to find ready accommodation at the students' halls of residence at the Baptist Seminary near to Rio's famous Sans Pena Praia. Aware of the dangers his friend Vicente faced of lapsing into the old pattern of drink and drugs if he remained in Amazonas alone, Bill invited Vicente to join him at the Seminary in Rio. They then would try to find a place in Rio for Vicente's wife and young son, Marcelo.

Accommodation was not easy to find in that area of Rio. One day a few weeks after Vicente's arrival, while they were still staying at the Baptist Seminary, they were aimlessly gazing out the window when suddenly they spied a removal van at an apartment block nearby. Hurriedly they rushed around to the place and discovered that the apartment was available although the rent would cost nearly everything they had in hand. Bill's friend, George Macedo, kindly — or maybe bravely, offered to be their guarantor. It was a step of faith, for they had no guaranteed income, but they took the key and moved in. A visit to the bank gave them an encouraging surprise when Bill found someone from Northern Ireland had sent a gift which was enough to pay the first month's rent.

Now that they were in possession of an apartment they sent for Vicente's family. They had absolutely no furniture so they slept on the floor and also had their meals sitting on the floor. Soon they began to acquire the basics. The day Vicente's wife, Patrice, arrived George Macedo kindly gave them his own mattress and a fridge. Bill's friend Wilki Baia who had studied with him and others on those late night sessions as students, loaned Bill enough money to buy two other mattresses for young Marcelo and himself.

Vicente got a job with the Baptist Publishing House, and while Bill was studying at the General Hospital he was able to secure himself some employment as a trainee ophthalmologist at various clinics around the city. It was barely enough to pay their rent, buy essential food and pay their bills.

Vicente worked hard at his job and was successful. Within a short time he was promoted to the position of Sales Manager. In the evenings he commenced a series of theological studies and as a result was invited to be a part-time pastor at a local Baptist church.

Meanwhile, Bill's studies continued unabated; he was learning in detail all the intricacies of ophthalmology and the skills of delicate surgery on the eye. He travelled two hours across Rio every day to the hospital and two hours back in the evenings. Bill admits that is was during those bus rides he did most of his study and memorisation.

Rio de Janeiro is undoubtedly one of the most beautiful cities in the world. The beautiful beaches of Copacobana, Leblom, Ipanema and Barra de Tijuca draw thousands of tourists from all over the world. The towering peaks of Pao de Acucar and Cocovado give outstanding views of the whole Guanabara Bay. The city seems to be constantly pervaded by an atmosphere of carnival and vacation. However, for Bill there was little time to indulge in the splendours of the beautiful city. His application to the work at hand paid off, and in due course Bill obtained the experience he needed for his diploma as a qualified ophthalmic surgeon.

In a prayer letter at that time Bill reported the following:

My time in the beautiful city of Rio has come to an end, and the purpose of my coming here has been accomplished. After graduation I moved to Rio to take a two year residency course in Ophthalmology leading on to specialisation in ophthalmic surgery. For a long time I found the surgical part of the course very difficult, but many of you prayed. For weeks I trained on pig's eyes... really quite sickening at first and I never want to look another pig straight in the eye. Today I am grateful for a steady hand and the confidence that comes through knowing that we can do all things through Him.

The "shoe making" projects all show great progress. Last year I was able to visit three of the four centres now making special shoes for the patients with leprosy. I was thrilled to see the results as I examined over one hundred patients using these shoes. One man had three ulcers on one foot and two on the other over a period of eleven years. As a result of the shoes he now has no ulcers even though he walks five kilometres to work every day.

In September last I was able to give a report on this work at the Congress of Dermatology held in the nation's capital, Brasilia. Each speaker was introduced "Professor So and So," but when it came to my turn the chairman simply said, "And now our beloved William." I am grateful to the Lord for the measure of acceptance with my Brazilian colleagues.

Let me also give you something for praise. A few days ago Vicente started his second year in the Baptist Seminary. He also continues working at the Baptist Publishing House and is director of Evangelism in his church. Just two years ago his life and home were ruined by drink. Praise the Lord for all He has done in this life. Thank you for helping me during these two years so that I can now help others also. What a difference it makes."

The course in Rio was now finished. Another goal had been reached. With his diploma in hand Bill's bags were packed and ready to go. Where? Now what?

Almost ten years had passed without a visit to Northern Ireland, and the news of his mother's health was not good. Nina, Bill's sister, had given up her employment at Robinson Cleaver's department store some years earlier to care for her mother. Everything indicated that a visit home was long overdue. First he had to travel back to Manaus to organise some matters before his planned trip to the United Kingdom. A phone call home to Nina before leaving Rio indicated that Mrs. Woods was in good form.

From Manaus he called home again the following weekend only to hear that his mother had passed away on the Thursday of that week. It seemed so ironic that when he was at last free to travel home his mother would no longer be there. His sister Nina assured him that all was well and not to rush his plans.

With the urgency taken out of his trip to Belfast Bill decided to travel home through Guinea Bissau in West Africa where he was able to visit the various works carried out by missionaries of the Worldwide Evangelisation Crusade (WEC). He was touched to see an even greater need than that he had already witnessed in Brazil. In the short time he was there he tried to help and encourage the dedicated missionaries. The frustration of seeing such great need in this Marxist West African State pulled heavily on his heart, and he wished he had another life to give for Africa and especially Guinea Bissau.

The visit to Africa gave Bill something more than he had expected. Not for the first time, he had picked up malaria which did not become evident until he arrived in Northern Ireland. Most people were expressing delight at the unusually fine spell of warm weather, but Bill could only shiver until his teeth chattered in the throes of a rigor. Soon afterwards the rigor gave way to profuse perspiring while his body ached with pain. Dr. Tom Gawley, who for some time had been a missionary in West Africa came to Bill's rescue with some anti-malarial medicine.

On arrival in Ulster Bill received news from Vicente and family in Rio de Janeiro:

I continue preaching in the prisons, in homes for down and outs and to drug addicts, and the Lord has been blessing my life and ministry. A friend from Northern Ireland sent a letter which quoted a verse from Deuteronomy reminding me that the Lord will keep us "as the apple of his eye." I used the verse in a message I preached, and at the close of the service my mother, my sister and my brother-in-law all came to the Lord. I am now starting my final year at Seminary and am acting as Vice Moderator and director of Evangelism for one of the largest Baptist Churches in Rio. Also at the seminary they have given me the responsibility as coordinator for evangelism. All this underlines not only the wonderful grace of God in my life, but also my need for your prayers and those of your friends.

Bill found that Northern Ireland had changed much since last he had been there. For ten years the country had been in the throes of political turmoil and terrorist attacks. Sunny Brazil had its problems with violence, but it was hard to come to terms with soldiers on the streets of Belfast and searches upon entering shops. Familiar landmarks had been destroyed, and it was hard to adapt again to the changeable weather patterns of Northern Ireland.

Nina was glad to see him again. Both his mother and father had passed away, and for the first few days he had to come to terms with these changes. Alex and Sadie were still in Northern Ireland, but Bob and his family were living in England while Brian, long since retired from the RAF, had taken a job as a consultant in Oman.

It was sweet to renew fellowship with many friends who had been standing behind Bill during all the former years. Dr. Paisley had moved into the new and larger Martyr's Memorial Free Presbyterian Church up the Ravenhill Road. Emma and Janet Munn whose testimony had inspired and stimulated him in his missionary career years before, were still at full stretch challenging and supporting missionaries. Roy and Dorothy Baird had kindly and faithfully looked after his practical interests during those ten years when he was absent.

It wasn't long before he was into a full itinerary of meetings all over the countryside. It was ironic that since his teenage years Bill had a driving license but had never learned to drive. He always had taken a bus or train to the location of the meetings when transport was not provided. Now he felt was the time to venture behind the wheel of a car. Sam McCallum gave him his first lessons in a small Morris Mini car in the grounds of the Martyrs Memorial Church. After a few lessons Bill concluded that the church was well built — at least it was still standing after several collisions against the outer walls of the new building.

Bill likes to recall the day he got the courage to drive the Mini into central Belfast unaccompanied by an instructor. All went well until it got to where he wanted to park the car. He slowly drove the Mini forward a few yards and halted. The car shivered like a lump of jelly as he started the revs to reverse into the vacant lot. Eventually the car moved back but didn't quite fit into the space nor near enough to the kerb. The vibration of the car was repeated again as he put pressure on the accelerator and tried to edge forward. Bill was getting nervous and a bit hot under the collar. These manoeuvres were repeated several times and in such a public place he felt every eye was glued on him.

Four soldiers had been observing Bill's performance from the rear of their army jeep. They could watch no longer so came over and invited him to get out of the car. Each soldier put his hands to a corner of the Mini and finally lifted it into the parking place. Bill was rather sheepish in expressing his thanks.

After gaining enough confidence and experience at driving he became more independent in his transport to and from meetings. However, he soon discovered that independence brought its own peculiar problems and predicaments. Returning very late one night from a meeting in the border town of Monaghan in the Republic of Ireland, Bill's car ran out of petrol in Lisburn, eight miles from home. He abandoned the car at the edge of the road and walked to a neighbouring hotel from where he phoned me at 1:20 a.m. to come to his rescue.

When he tried to return to the car, he found the whole area cordoned off by the security forces. A soldier told him he could not proceed because a suspicious car had been abandoned near to the entrance of the Army Headquarters for Northern Ireland. Bill would have to wait until they carried out a controlled explosion on the car which would render the area safe. When Bill enquired what the suspicious car was like the soldier started to describe the red Mini car Bill had just abandoned. Embarrassingly he admitted the car was his and explained his dilemma. In the interrogation that followed the soldiers told him at what time he had crossed the Monaghan border and wanted to know his movements since then. He had quite a job to convince them that the car was his own and not only did he lose direction going home so late at night, but in trying to find the right way home he ran out of petrol.

He was released only when one of the soldier interrogators questioned Bill about being a missionary and asked if he knew a missionary named John Brown. Bill replied in the affirmative and volunteered that John was a missionary in India with Operation Mobilisation. With this satisfactory answer, not only was the army operation to carry out a controlled explosion aborted, Bill was also spared having to pay a heavy fine.

A few minutes later I arrived with a gallon of petrol for his car. Bill was still quite excited and tried to explain to me how John Brown had just saved his skin. I couldn't understand how that could be, for I knew John Brown was in India.

At the Belfast's Royal Victoria Hospital's Ophthalmic Unit Professor Desmond Archer kindly permitted Bill to attend the ophthalmic clinics and surgeries to gain further clinical experience. Mr. Trevor Buchannon, one of Professor Archer's leading surgeons, took Bill under his wing and instructed him in many useful techniques. The year spent there was an enriching experience that proved invaluable on his return to Brazil. Over and above the profitable experience Bill also gained many friends among the staff and patients at the hospital. Both Professor Archer and Mr Buchannon continued to take an active interest in Bill's progress on the other side of the world.

As well as the valuable training gained at the Royal Victoria Hospital in Belfast Bill also spent a month in Dublin where he gained the Diploma in Ophthalmology at The Royal College of Surgeons. He attended further courses at the New York Eye and Ear Hospital

Medical College where he was greatly helped by Dr. Pierre Guiboi of Park Avenue, New York.

During that year Audrey and I were finishing a five year assignment at the home end of Acre Gospel Mission before we left to live for a few years in the United States. We were glad to be able to share in many meetings with Bill in Ulster and England during that year at home. It was a particular pleasure and blessing to have Bill re-instated as a full member of the Acre Gospel Mission after the prolonged leave of absence.

A year slips by very quickly when one is busy. Bill had been stocking up on medical and surgical equipment for some time in anticipation of the new programme he would have to set up in Brazil on his return. Some new equipment was purchased with donations kindly given by both churches and individuals, and the rest was either discarded and obsolete equipment donated by local hospitals or acquired from the Missionary Medical Supplies at Echo in Putney near London.

Chapter Twenty

A New Beginning

❖

In November 1978 Bill left Northern Ireland for a short course at the Scheiffelin Leprosy Research Sanatorium in South India. Besides benefiting greatly from the course and the expertise of those who performed the reconstructive surgery on leprosy patients Bill was also overwhelmed by the poverty and need of so many on the Indian sub-continent. Again he felt the same challenge about India as he had faced in Africa. But his future work was in Brazil. On return from India he spent a brief time in Northern Ireland and then flew back to Brazil via the United States.

A matter Bill constantly had before him in prayer was where the Lord would have him work on his return. Brazil is a big country. The need was great and the opportunities were many. Dr. Samuel Cukierman, who owns a large private clinic in the magnificent Rio de Janeiro, not only offered Bill a place to work with him at the clinic but also to pay for any further training Bill might want to take in Ophthalmics. Dr. Cukierman was most annoyed and disappointed when Bill turned down this very attractive and lucrative offer.

The leprosy programme all over the country was in great need. Many states in Brazil would have been glad to contract Bill for their leprosy programme. Several British and American agencies which have work in Brazil also wanted to recruit him to their ranks. The offers were tempting. George Macedo would like to have had his services at the leprsoy unit near Rio de Janeiro where Bill's good friend Dr. Eduardo from his days in Boca do Acre was now the Secretary of Health for the state. Professor Sinsio Talhari was keen that Bill go to work in Manaus as were other friends at the Dermatology Clinic Alfredo da Matta in Manaus. Dr. Tom Geddis, Bill's colleague in the Acre Gospel Mission, was sure there was a place for him in Acre where his skills were greatly needed.

It was not a matter of being torn between the beautiful beaches of Rio de Janeiro with its inviting moderate climate as opposed to the steamy heat of the remote isolation of the Acre — for Bill the priority was to know and do the will of God. Discovering God's will is neither a shot in the dark nor a step of chance. Bill carefully weighed things up and talked to the Lord in prayer asking His direction for the way ahead.

Dr. Ademir, the head of Brazil's National Leprosy Programme and a good friend from Bill's days in Rio, sent him to Belem, the state capital of Paraáand the city right at the mouth of the River Amazon. It seemed to Bill to be the right step to take. He had already seen first hand the tremendous need in that area from the days when he set up the first boot workshop for Leprosy sufferers in the State of Para. Convinced in his mind that this was the direction he should follow, Bill sent all his belongings a thousand miles down river from Manaus. On arrival in Belem he took temporary accommodation with Edmund and Marie Norwood, missionaries serving with UFM from Northern Ireland.

Soon after his arrival in Belem he submitted his medical qualifications for local registration and waited for the completion of this process. The registration was delayed for quite some time. Bill became restless in his heart about the delay. In the interim he decided to return to Manaus and from there to proceed to visit Tom and Ethel Geddis in Tarauaca which was almost three thousand miles west from Belem. En route to visit Tom and Ethel in Tarauaca Bill had to make a scheduled stop at Cruzeiro do Sul. This was the first time he had visited Cruzeiro, Acre's most remote and second largest city and he was stranded there while waiting for an ongoing flight to the neighbouring town of Tarauaca. Those few unplanned days in Cruzeiro impressed on him the need of the leprsoy programme in the town.

On arrival at Tarauaca he found that Tom was due to leave on a Missionary Aviation Fellowship flight to Rio Branco the state capital, and Tom invited Bill to join him on the trip. In the Acre capital Tom introduced Bill to the Secretary of Health for the state, Dr. Labib Murad, who on hearing of Bill's interest and commitment to a leprosy programme immediately offered him a position in Cruzeiro do Sul. Having been so recently impressed by what he had seen in that city Bill felt this was God's hand definitely leading him in this direction.

He wasted no time returning to Belem where he withdrew the application for registration and dispatched his unopened equipment and baggage by river steamer for his new address in far off Cruzeiro do Sul. The boat left Belem early in May and did not arrive in Cruzeiro until September. It ran aground on the River Juru and was consequently delayed. Bill was glad to finally be re-united with his personal belongings and equipment. Without the latter he was greatly curtailed in his work

Acre, Brazil's smallest state and yet larger than Great Britain. already had the reputation as being the "Leprosy State" with eleven people in every 1,000 of the population afflicted with the disease. Cruzeiro do Sul which drew its patients from all parts of the Juruá Valley including some neighbouring towns in Amazonas, had the highest incidence of leprosy in the whole state with twenty-five people in every 1,000 citizens suffering from leprosy. The World Health Organisation's appraisal of endemic leprosy regions is when more than 0.1 people in every 1000 are infected with the disease. Leprosy in Cruzeiro do Sul was undeniably a major problem.

Apart from his recent unscheduled stop-over in Cruzeiro do Sul Bill had never been to the city and most certainly had not even enquired about living conditions or the situation that prevailed in the local hospital and clinic. This required another step of faith which the Lord honoured. The state government offered Bill a salary paid contract which gave him the wherewithal to survive. Initially he stayed in a hotel until he was able to move to rented property. At the hospital his arrival was greatly welcomed by the para-medic Antonio Barahuma, better known locally as "Dr. Courage," who tended to the leprosy patients in the town.

Bill's first task was to appraise the whole situation, examine the patients already registered and verify their treatment and the degree of deformities of each patient. In the process of registration and examination Bill was surprised to meet up with two former friends. Pastor Miquel whom Bill had befriended and diagnosed as a leprosy sufferer while at the Baptist Seminary in Manaus, was now pastoring a church in Carauari, four days down river from Cruzeiro. His assistant pastor was Joao Batista whom Bill first diagnosed as a patient in Canutama.

Having affirmed the treatment and progress of each registered patient, Bill majored on corrective surgery for deformed limbs to restore a measure of mobility. He was greatly restricted by the lack of ophthalmic equipment to perform the eye surgery which was also needed by so many. His friend George Macedo put Bill in touch with several orthopaedic surgeons who visited Cruzeiro do Sul and performed operations on the most needy patients. Dr. Waldemar Lopes, a plastic surgeon Bill had known during his time in Rio de Janeiro, travelled from the other end of Brazil to Cruzeiro on two occasions where his skills were put to good use on Bill's patients. The irony of Dr. Waldemar's visits to Cruzeiro do Sul to benefit its populace was tragically underscored some years later when his son Richard, as co-pilot on a Vasp cargo plane, was killed in an air disaster as they attempted a night landing a Cruzeiro do Sul.

Besides working at the hospital and travelling on the surrounding rivers to meet his patients, Bill got greatly involved at the local Faith Baptist Church, and he enjoyed the fellowship and ministry of Pastor Jader. Before long he was sharing the ministry of the Word on alternate weeks with the pastor.

After a two year spell in Cruzeiro, Bill travelled to the United States and India to develop his experience on the techniques of reconstructive surgery for the rehabilitation of limbs and also to secure more equipment for his work. Through the kindness and generosity of friends in Northern Ireland he was able to purchase a portable operating microscope to help in the ophthalmic micro surgery of his patients

The newly learned techniques plus the equipment acquired greatly enhanced Bill's work in Cruzeiro do Sul. Many of those who had been blinded as a result of chronic scarring to their eyes were restored to sight by the micro surgery Bill performed with the help of the new operating microscope. There must be few tasks in life more satisfying than being able to restore sight to a sightless person. Further surgery was also done to the eyelids renewing the simple but important function of blinking which besides protecting the eye also constantly cleans and lubricates it.

Shortly after returning to Cruzeiro Bill did not know there was a surprise waiting for him. The reputation of his surgery and how well the leprosy programme had been organised in Cruzeiro soon got to the state capital, and Bill was invited by the Secretary of Health to go to Rio Branco and take the position as the Co-ordinator of the Leprosy Programme for the whole state. The overall programme across the state was in a precarious condition.

Besides praying about this matter Bill also visited Tom and Ethel Geddis in the neighbouring town of Tarauaca to seek their counsel. To everyone it seemed to be the obvious move, for the situation in Acre demanded it, and Bill had both the surgical and administrative skills to make it work. Besides, Bill remembered his visit to the Leprosarium the first time he visited Rio Branco eighteen years earlier. He never could forget the look of despair on the patients and the sense of hopelessness that pervaded the place. He remembered also his prayer to the Lord asking for help. Now the Lord was opening the door to answer that prayer.

Although the transfer to Rio Branco seemed to be the right decision, it was nonetheless resented and resisted by the people of Cruzeiro do Sul. So great was the disappointment locally that the town council convened a special meeting in an attempt to retain this doctor whom they had come to love and respect. As a result of that meeting the council chairman sent the following letter to the Secretary of Health in Rio Branco:

25/03/81 Senhor Secretario

The mission of a councillor is always to seek the welfare of the city he represents. It is for this reason I am writing this letter so that you may attend to a matter which was raised at our last council meeting. It is already commented here in Cruzeiro that the Secretary of Health has plans for the future transfer to the Acre Capital the competent and dedicated Dr. William John Woods. He has rendered invaluable service to the leprosy patients of our city, treating them with true love and esteem and is without a doubt a true slave of his profession. We would therefore be grateful if you would permit him to stay with us for a longer time.
We ask you to give this request this your full consideration.

Sincerely,
Lyrio Eduardo de Azevedo Chairman of Council Cruzeiro do Sul

To this letter the State Secretary of Health replied:

23/04/81 Senhor Chairman,

In reply to your letter we wish to inform you that William John Woods will not be taken away from his functions in Cruzeiro do Sul, but by his praiseworthy work in the treatment of the victims of leprosy he will be promoted to the important post of state coordinator of the leprosy programme with responsibility for the whole state.
I would like to point out that Acre has the highest incidence of leprosy in all Brazil, and for that reason the Ministry of Health decided to widen the front in the war against this stigmatised disease. To effect this undertaking we need Dr. William to be available for the whole state including Cruzeiro do Sul where he will frequently

be required because of the great need that exists there. In taking this action the Ministry would like to have the understanding of the people in your town and also the local council as to our motives in transferring this doctor who has earned such great respect locally. It is important to recognise that Dr. Woods' contribution instead of decreasing will actually be expanded.

I trust we can count on the cooperation and help of you all in the battle to eradicate the stigma of Hansens disease in our state.

We send our sincere greetings
Dr. Labib Murad Secretary of Health

Dr. Labib Murad who was then the Secretary of Health is today the vice-governor of Acre and still is an enthusiastic supporter of Bill's work.

Rio Branco is a frontier town in Acre which borders Bolivia and Peru. Until the great Trans-Amazon highway was opened up in the 1970s the city was remote and isolated. With the opening of the highway this previously small and inert town, where life had been so easy going, suddenly took on the features of real city life. There was rapid growth and development. Industry and commerce greatly expanded as firms from the sout¹ of Brazil took advantage of government subsidies to help develop the Acre economy. There was also steady migration from the southern cities as well as from the interior towns and surrounding forest to the city. Housing projects provided small, medium and luxury homes for the increasing population. Deforestation became a global issue as land was cleared to make room for large farms. Sadly, as always with such growth, gangsterism and crime greatly increased in Rio Branco making the streets a perilous place after night fall.

With the mushrooming of the economy, industry and housing were increasing. Sadly many sufferers of leprosy were left behind as people jumped on the bandwagon looking for a better life. When Bill arrived in Rio Branco his official position was General

Coordinater for the control of leprosy in the Acre State. The job description did not reveal just how serious and uncontrolled the disease was, and many of the city's inhabitants became alarmed as the numbers of leprosy sufferers began to soar in their area.

In two years Bill had been able to establish and organise the leprosy program in Cruzeiro do Sul, and he was shocked upon his arrival in Rio Branco to find his new department in total disarray. The small team contracted by the government and allocated to the work was dispirited and without goals or objectives. Nurse Ruth Rodriques remembers that the official file and record of patients amounted to a pile of papers in a cardboard soap box. The driver of the department's only vehicle knew more about the location and condition of the patients than the rest of the team, and he had just left the leprosy programme to work elsewhere. It was not just a matter of starting from the bottom rung, Bill felt like he was starting from below the bottom rung. The programme would need all the qualities of someone who had discipline, determination and dedication to do the job. All these qualities were found in Bill Woods.

At first they had to search for and then examine all the patients that were known to the small team and establish their treatment. Proper records were prepared of these, and case histories kept of their disease and any resulting deformities. Having assessed those who were the obvious cases, a programme of visitation took place in the city to discover how many other patients there were, who was on treatment and if there were secondary deformities with the disease. As the assessments were made Bill had to train the staff on how to keep proper records of each patient. To provide accommodation for these files he had to argue his case to the hospital's authorities to assign him offices for the necessary administration. The general perception in all departments was that leprosy cases should be treated at the leprosy colony out of town and not at the dermatology department of the hospital. To do this would have added further stigma and hardship to the patients, and Bill insisted it was important they have ready access to the General Hospital.

Soon the number of patients wanting consultations grew rapidly to the extent that there was insufficient room for them at the out-patient consulting room. Again Bill had to convince the hospital management that he needed more space to carry out his programme. After much wrangling and many requests that were repeatedly refused or deferred, this extra space was finally granted. Check-ups and patient evaluation continued, and soon Bill concluded that there were sufferers of leprosy who could be controlled with chemotherapy as out patients. Others needed prolonged attention in the wards, and still others needed corrective surgery. Still Bill had to present his case further to be given access to an operating theatre where these operations could be effected. Reluctantly this also was given.

Bill's persistence in fighting for the programme helped bind the small and previously discouraged group into a tightly knit team. Dr. Leia Borges had joined the leprosy programme in 1979. She was on maternity leave when Bill arrived in 1982, but she soon returned to augment Bill's support. Dr. Clara whom Bill had known at university in Manaus and whose husband was the pastor of the church Bill attended, was a very dedicated worker. Emily Gilchrist from Northern Ireland who had been a missionary nurse with SIM International at the famous Vom Hospital in Jos, Nigeria, brought much needed experience and compassionate skill to the programme. Nurse Maria Socorro Brasiliense arrived from Brasilia and was an invaluable and dedicated member of the staff. In the event of Bill's absence she acted as a very efficient coordinator of the local leprosy programme and was as vital as Bill's right arm in all his work. Nurse Rute Rodriques was a devoted worker for her patients as were nurses Vania, Conceicao, Pastora, Gloria and Rose. They were all inspired by Bill's crusading spirit to make sure things happened for the benefit of the patients. Writing in the Rio Branco Gazeta, Rio Branco's leading daily newspaper, Socorro Brasiliense admitted, "We form one family made up of doctors, nurses, drivers, para-medics and patients."

Having assessed and examined all the patients they could find in the greater Rio Branco area and prescribed the necessary treatment, a long list of operations was drawn up for correction of hands that were palsied by the disease and dropped feet which patients trailed when they tried to walk. Added to this, many eye operations were necessary to restore sight to blinded eyes. Facial surgery was also required to compensate for damaged nerves which controlled the eye lids.

To help with this daunting task Bill appealed to his old friend George Macedo for assistance. George again drew on the resources in CERPHA and was able to arrange for several surgeons to visit Rio Branco, not only to perform the operations, but also to train local surgeons in the Acre in various surgical skills and techniques. Dr. Frank Deurkson came from Canada, and with great expertise not only carried out corrective surgery on some of Bill's most needy patients, but also mentored Dr. Alvaro, a local orthopaedic surgeon who took part in those operations and began to learn the new surgical procedures for these intricate operations in transpositioning tendons to compensate for those that had lost their use as a result of the disease. Dr. Duerkson's visits were followed by those of Dr. Marcos Virmond from the Bauru Leprosy Centre in Sao Paulo. He also did intricate surgery and passed on his experience and skills to Dr. Alvaro and Bill. Sadly at times limbs that were beyond remedy or recovery had to be amputated.

The programme was very much a team work. Nurses Emily Gilchrist and Maria Socorro Brasiliense not only gave compassionate and sensitive care to the patients, but Rose, a physiotherapist, came to teach them the benefits of physiotherapy. Surgery without physical rehabilitation for limbs that long had been useless would be of little effect. Special exercises were necessary both before and after surgery. Legs and feet, arms and hands were steeped in wax, simple movements were encouraged and individual supervision was given to each patient.

Slide presentations were prepared and used to educate the patients and their families about leprosy and so helped eradicate much of the ignorance and superstition that prevailed about the disease. The progress was painstakingly slow, but it began to pay dividends. Nurse Pastora said, "During my eight years working with the team I have been humbled and made happy. I have seen patients cry with despair when they were diagnosed as positive and it was confirmed they had leprosy. It is a traumatic experience. I have witnessed the same patients weep again with relief and gratitude when they have been declared healed."

Picture the sad but not uncommon plight of a man who is blinded by leprosy and has secondary deformities to his limbs with the result being that the appendages at the end of his arms are but useless stumps. Writing and reading are impossible. How about eating a meal? He cannot see where the plate is or where the food is. He has no hands to hold a spoon or a fork, and with an insensitive stump of a hand he cannot feel if the cup is hot or cold.

Bill explains, "If you want to know something of what their predicament is like, close your eyes and try to find or lift a spoon with your elbow—while you still have your coat on." Deprived of the vital senses of sight and touch and with deformed feet which are virtually useless, the patient is a total prisoner of his disease. An added hazard is that rats and cockroaches often gnaw at the desensitised fingers and feet. For this very reason it is important that leprosy patients be encouraged to have a cat to protect their limbs from these vermin.

Can you imagine the joy of a patient when after surgery and weeks of exercise he is able to take his first steps without having to consciously lift his leg high enough to avoid trailing his foot? Think of the woman who previously was unable to do such a simple thing as to hold a knife and fork or feed herself with a spoon but now is independent of being spoon fed. Picture the man or woman who could not see to eat who, now with the benefit of surgery and aid of glasses, can now see what they are eating. The blind victim of leprosy who cannot even appreciate the touch of his hand on his son's head or on his daughter's cheek can now, after surgery, see his children. Other patients whose limbs are too badly deformed and could not benefit from restoration surgery and therapy are taught how to hold a spoon in the stump of a hand and secure the utensil with an elastic band. Simple things? Maybe, but they make life all so different.

In 1983 Bill wrote of one patient who had been blind for fourteen years:

She was so maimed by leprosy that she even had to have the food put in her mouth. Without feeling in her hands she could not locate a spoon on the table nor even a handle on the door. After surgery she has 60% vision and is excited that she can feed herself and go to the bathroom unattended.

Bill related another account of a patient in Manaus:

Sr. Major is a lovely believer who lives a Antonio Aleixo. Our missionaries visit with him regularly, and on these visits he loves to sing. Sadly, Sr. Major for seventeen years was never able to see his visitors. Worse still, he was not able to see his food, and in his blind condition and without feeling in his hands, he was not able to find his spoon or even locate his food. Through ophthalmic surgery we have given Sr. Major the simple luxury of being able to see his family, his friends and his food and made him less dependant on those who previously had to feed him.

Jose Eudes was one of the first patients to have an operation to correct the typically deformed "claw-hammer hand." Writing of him at the time Bill reported:

Today we did an operation on a twenty-two year old boy's hand. The first operation restored movement to the thumb, and then today's surgery will enable the other four fingers to regain their mobility. It was only yesterday when I went into his room to tell him about the time of the operation that I realised what a struggle he had to hold his knife and fork. I know that after this operation he will be able to make a better job of eating.

It seemed at the time Jose's was an experimental operation. Tendons were spliced and repositioned to compensate for the atrophied muscles damaged by leprosy. For cosmetic purposes a silicone implant replaced the cavity created by the wasted muscle between the base of the index finger and the base of the thumb. Although it was a pioneer effort, for the team the operation seemed to be a success.

Some weeks after his discharge from the hospital Bill spoke to Jose on a follow up visit and asked, "What has changed most in your life since your surgery?"

An embarrassed smile broke on his face, "I don't have to wait for my mother to button my shirt in the mornings." Following the initial sessions of physiotherapy Jose went missing from Rio Branco and was not heard of again for many years.

As the leprosy programme developed, news of its success in Acre spread to the neighbouring Brazilian states which also faced a similar crisis coping with the treatment of leprosy patients in their areas.

To help these states a symposium on reconstructive surgery was arranged in Porto Velho, the capital of Rondonia which is also part of the Amazon basin. Medical authorities from all over Brazil attended including Dr. Maria Leide Oliveira from Brasilia, the brilliant coordinator for Brazil's National Leprsoy Programme. The event presented the news of the progress that had been made by the team in Rio Branco which had transformed what had previously been a desperate situation in Acré. News of this symposium was broadcast on local radio and television.

Unknown to Bill, Jose Eudes was now living in Porto Velho, and when he heard on the television about the symposium and of Dr. Bill's presence at it, he decided to make an appearance even though he had not been invited. He knew that some of the team who operated on him years earlier would be there, and he wanted them to know how grateful he was. The Rio Branco contingent were not only surprised to see him, but they could not have had a better demonstration of the success of their surgical work than Jose offered them that day.

After close examination of his hand by the doctors present Jose told them that he had gained a new confidence following his operation because noone even suspected he suffered from leprosy. The surgery had not only restored mobility to his hands but had eliminated the stigma of the "claw hammer hand" that inevitably would have classified him in society as a sufferer of leprosy. Dr. Maria Leide, the national coordinator for the whole of Brazil, was greatly impressed.

Subsequent to his surgery Jose secured a good job in Porto Velho without being detected that he had been a eprosy patient. Also, because of the symposium, Dr. Cabral, a Brazilian Christian surgeon, was motivated to dedicate his skills and energies to the setting up of a similar leprosy programme in his home state of Rondonia. That assignment continues to this day under Dr. Cabral's leadership and with the cooperation of a Dutch leprosy team.

One common misconception about leprosy is that it only affects people on the lower social scale, the poor and ill nourished. This is not necessarily the case. Numbered among Bill's patients are politicians, European and American missionaries, bank managers, business men, fellow doctors, priests, pastors, teachers, university professors and other professionals. Countless others are ordinary men and women, children and adolescents. They come from every walk of life, and unwittingly they have become infected with the disease. Leprosy is no respector of persons.

Chapter Twenty-One

A Big Step Forward

❖

It should be said that conditions at the General Hospital in the centre of Rio Branco were far from acceptable and often shocked those medical professionals who came from other parts of Brazil or from the United States. It was a well known and established fact which was published in national newspapers and magazines throughout Brazil, that often patients in the Rio Branco Hospital had their insensitive toes or fingers gnawed at by rodents in the night. Even by day rats could be seen in the hospital grounds. However, Bill believed it was better to work with what he had than not to do any work at all. Only when the state governor visited the hospital and was appalled to see vermin race down a corridor were steps taken to eradicate them

Emily Gilchrist wrote of her arrival at the hospital in Rio Branco:

When I arrived in October 1982, Ruth Rodriques, who was to become my very good friend, was the only nurse providing any patient care. She was a dedicated Christian and was so loving with the patients. I was introduced to her on my first day at the hospital, and she took me on a tour of the building. When I saw the conditions in which I would have to work my initial reaction was to run away. However, I knew the Lord had brought me to these people, so I prayed and asked the Lord for grace and help. It was then that I proved by experience what the Lord said to Paul, "My grace is sufficient for you."

One morning some of the patients thought it would be quite a joke to frighten me by catching a rat and tying it to the leg of one of the beds for my arrival. It was not so much the fright they gave me, (and believe me they did!) but these same rats invaded the hospital at night and did a lot of damage. One patient named Betsie woke up one morning to find her bed sheets covered in blood. During the night a rat had chewed at one of her insensitive feet and caused a profuse haemorrhage.

In 1985 Bill was made director of the hospital for one year during which he introduced great changes on a very limited budget. Emily wrote for the Acre Missionary News:

Conditions have changed dramatically after Dr. Bill's arrival, and the hospital is now a different place. Not only did Bill greatly improve the care and treatment of the patients but also the conditions in the hospital. One of the first jobs was to employ a man to fill in all the holes in walls, floors and bathrooms where the rats had been entering. Some walls were tiled and others painted to improve hygiene and appearance.

At first we had only twelve beds for our patients, and this was far too few for the numbers of patients who needed long term treatment and care. Bill was able to increase our capacity to thirty beds and thus relieve the back log of patients who needed urgent attention. Bill was made director of the BASE Hospital for one year, and this gave him opportunity to introduce many general improvements throughout the hospital.

Our patients come from all over the Acre and from many towns in the neighbouring state of Amazonas. Officially we are not responsible for those outside our state, but morally we cannot turn them away. A team of young men was recruited and trained to find those in each Acre town and interior region who suffer from leprosy.

They visit schools and isolated settlements and forest homes to teach how to recognise the disease and how to begin preventative care. Most of these workers in the towns and on the rivers are Christians, and they also conduct meetings wherever they go. Already we have more than 10,000 leprosy patients registered and receiving treatment, and we believe many more are yet to be traced.

Another patient who came to live in Rio Branco to be near Dr. Bill and the team was Joao from Canutama. He was the young man whose hand had stuck to the hot metal plate without him feeling the searing burns. Joao had since married and set up home in Rio Branco where he was converted to the Gospel of Jesus Christ. Today he is healed from his leprosy and is a faithful believer and loyal church member.

Besides the medical and surgical programme, each morning Emily Gilchrist and Ruth Rodriques went from ward to ward and gave the patients daily devotions from the Word of God. Most operations were performed in the mornings, but in the afternoon Emily would often visit her patients again just to befriend them, listen to their problems, advise them, read and pray with them and often lead them to personal faith in Jesus Christ.

Of this work Nurse Gilchrist said, "Many of our patients are dejected and often feel rejected by friends and family. For these we have good news—Christ loves them and will never leave them when they give their heart and life to Him." Emily was instrumental in leading many of the patients to personal faith in Jesus Christ. One of those patients whom Emily led to faith in Christ was not only healed and discharged from the programme, but today he is the pastor of a small church in his interior town. Because the Lord had freed him from the despair that leprosy had previously brought to his life, he wanted to dedicate the rest of his life to serve the Saviour.

In close conjunction with the leprosy programme at the hospital there was the vital contribution made by the German missionary Ursula Milhan and her team at the shoe and limb workshop. Here patients, referred from the hospital for shoes or limbs, were assessed as to the extent of their deformities. Accordingly either shoes, sandals, boots or limbs were prepared and fitted. Parallel bars were used to help educate immobilised patients to walk again with their newly acquired mechanical limbs. The workshop had all the activity of a busy factory. The skilled workmen who operated the machines had a special interest in their work — they were all former leprosy patients.

Little by little the regular visits of surgeons coming to Rio Branco and the routine operations of Dr. Alvaro and Dr. Bill, made a great transformation on the patients in the capital. However, out in the smaller towns throughout the state there were isolated people who live scattered throughout the jungle. Bill asked the question, "What could be done for them?"

For almost twenty years Bill travelled thousands of miles, sometimes on single and twin engine planes that had a reputation of regularly falling out of the sky. He tried to be prudent about these flights, and the Lord has been gracious in protecting his life while many others have sadly crashed in the forest with high loss of life.

In each town Bill encouraged the local authorities to appoint a responsible person to represent the leprosy programme locally. Dr. Geddis in Tarauaca assisted Bill in various operations at the small hospital in the town. Cases that could not be resolved locally were taken to Rio Branco, many of them at Bill's personal expense, where they were interned and prepared for surgery. After surgery and post-operative physiotherapy and providing they were sufficiently rehabilitated, the patients returned to their home towns.

The portable operating microscope and slit lamp Bill had acquired some years earlier were put to good use not only in his travels in Acre but he also made frequent visits to Manaus in cooperation with the work of Dr. Sinesio and the friends at the Alfredo da Matta Clinic. Many diseased and deformed patients at the Colonia Antonio Aleixo were greatly helped by the frequent visits Bill made and the operations he performed there.

Occasionally Bill and some of his team would be called on to make a "Mercy Mission" to some isolated and needy area. On these errands of compassion the portable operating microscope was invaluable. One such incident was when an appeal came from Canutama where Bill first felt constrained to embark on his career to relieve the suffering of leprosy patients. Dona Francisca, the elderly wife of Old Joao Bizerra, the boatsman who made many trips on the various tributaries with Bill and Jack Mawdsley, due to mature cataracts on her eyes, had lost her sight. Old Joao was already dead, all her children were married and had left home. Dona Francisca was not only depressed in her loneliness and poverty, but with the added loss of vision she lived in physical darkness and life itself seemed bleak. The family heard that Bill had operated on many such patients with great success and wanted him to help her.

When the appeal reached Bill he felt he owed it to Dona Francisca to try and help. However, there were formidable obstacles which made this difficult. Canutama was not only far away, it was one of the most inaccessible towns in the Amazon Valley. It had no regular air service, and to travel there by boat would take at least two weeks beside the time spent treating the patient. Dona Francisca's general health made it impossible for her to travel to Rio Branco or Manaus.

Bill asked Nurse Socorro Brasiliense if she would volunteer as part of a team to travel to Canutama. It would involve flying one hour by commercial jet to Porto Velho where they would hire the single engine plane and pilot from the Wycliffe Bible Translators to fly them an hour and a half over dense jungle to Canutama. Socorro was due holidays and planned to spend that time in Brasilia with her family. However, always willing to help, she offered to stop off at Porto Velho early in the day on her way through to Brasilia and travel over to Canutama to assist Bill with the operation provided she could return in the afternoon to continue her trip south to the capital on the evening flight. It was a tight schedule, but Bill felt it could be done and was worth the effort.

Bill sent word to Canutama and marked a date for Dona Francisca's operation. Not only were instructions given on what preparations were to be made, but he requested a suitable place where they might perform the surgery as there was no hospital in the town. On the pre-arranged day the commercial flight to Porto Velho was delayed which added pressure to their timetable. As soon as the jet touched down they changed planes into a small single engine aircraft and were soon airborne again over the jungle.

At the simple clay airstrip in Canutama Dona Francisca's family met and escorted them to a small clinic near the centre of town. Dona Francisca walked up the hill from her house to the clinic. The team scrubbed down for operation. The patient lay on a makeshift surgical table. Soon the operation was underway.

When they finished surgery they had to wait for the old lady to recover sufficiently from the anaesthetic before they could remove her from the room as the stretcher could not be negotiated round the narrow door way. Finally when they got her on her feet they accompanied her as she walked back to her son's house—a simple wooden structure nearby.

During the closing moments of the operation the pilot kept reminding them that darkness would soon fall, and they might miss Socorro's on-going flight; if they delayed too long, they would have to remain in Canutama until the following day. With Dona Francisca safely returned to her family and already requesting food, Socorro rushed to the air strip where the pilot already had the engine running. The small plane vibrated fiercely as it gathered speed over the hard clay runway. On the ground friends waved their farewells to Socorro who responded from the plane as it lifted off. Soon she was climbing above the late afternoon clouds and on her way back to Porto Velho. Thankfully, she was on time to catch the evening flight to Brasilia as planned and continue her vacation. Bili remained in Canutama for several days.

The programme was not without its disappointments and set backs. The work received a harsh blow in 1988 when Emily Gilchrist, who had made a vital contribution to the success of the work, announced she would not be able to return to Brazil. Everyone was happy to hear of her wedding back in Northern Ireland, but they were also disappointed because such a valuable worker would not be returning to Brazil.

Another reversal came when a thief or thieves broke into Bill's consulting room and stole his slit lamp. The lamp was not only expensive, in Rio Branco it was irreplaceable. Operations and examinations were stopped for quite a while until another lamp was finally acquired from the United Kingdom. A bigger insult followed when a person in Rio Branco, acting as a friend, suggested to Bill that for a sum of money he knew where the slit lamp could be bought back from the thieves who had stolen it.

In 1988 after the team had lost the immense contribution of Emily Gilchrist, Bill felt it was time to assess what had been accomplished and what was yet to be done. At that time two things happened that were to greatly enhance their programme and make a greater impact on the leprosy scourge in the Acre.

While their projects and plans were on schedule, it was agreed to use the Multidrug Therapy (MDT). This treatment was first introduced by the World Health Organisation in 1981. As the name Multidrug Treatment suggests, it is a combined regimen of three drugs which are taken together. To administer the treatment it was necessary to have a well planned and a properly controlled programme. First experimented with in Malta, the MDT had been used with great success in India, Pakistan and various countries in Africa.

The authorised use of the Multidrug Therapy in Brazil was only permitted at first at the Curipaiti Leprosy Hospital in Rio de Janeiro where Dr. Maria Leide supervised its use. Shortly afterwards Bill's friend Dr. Sensio also had authority to use MDT at the Alfredo da Matta Clinic in Manaus. A study was done in Rio to find out if the MDT programme were feasible—would the patients come every month to receive the treatment. In Manaus a study was carried out to see if the MDT was effective in bringing about a cure for the patients.

In 1988 the Ministry of Health permitted the gradual introduction of MDT to other parts of the country. During that year Bill agreed to work as a MDT supervisor for the Ministry of Health in Brazil's north eastern cities of Recife and Maceió. While he was there the national coordinator of Brazil's Leprosy Programme, his friend Dr. Maria Leide de Oliveira, contacted Bill and asked him to return to Rio Branco and prepare a project for the introduction of MDT in Acre.

This was great news for Bill and a tremendous challenge. He presented a paper in which he argued and appealed for Rio Branco to be also included as a centre permitted to use the MDT. This paper with full documentation of their work was carefully prepared.

Just then two Italians representing an Overseas Aid Programme of the Italian Government were in Brasilia. Dr. Silvano Renzo and Sr. Trevisan had travelled all over Brazil looking for a place to start their contribution to the fight against lprosy. They were shown the paper Bill had presented to Brasilia and were very impressed by the need of the area and the work being done by Bill's team.

Dr. Silvano Renzo, an Italian surgeon with wide experience in leprosy programmes in Africa, decided to take a closer look at what was happening in Rio Branco. When he arrived he saw first hand how efficiently the programme was working, the dedication of the team, Bill's conscientious leadership and his modest appeal for help. All this, together with the obvious need of the region, moved Dr. Renzo to enlarge Bill's original estimate of what was needed to help. He strongly recommended his government's agency to seriously consider the Acre region as a fertile place for their proposed programme in Brazil

Dr. Renzo's recommendation was accepted, but the Italian delegation decided to focus on Cruzeiro do Sul which had the infamy of having the highest incidence of leprosy in Latin America. The result was that the Italian Overseas Aid Programme for the control of Leprosy in the Acre amounted to considerable financial commitment. A team of doctors and surgeons were assigned to a three year programme to combat leprosy in the Acre.

Spearheading this project with the Italians demanded a lot of administration. Included in Bill's plans to help combat leprosy in Acre was the recruitment of small teams of workers in each Acre town where canoes were made available, and enough resources were given to enable them to visit all the centres at the river edge and back into the forest. On these trips every home in the interior had to be visited, examination made of children and adults, leprosy sufferers registered and the treatment initiated.

The new MDT medicine had to be administered once a month, and the patient was required to take the tablets in the presence of a nurse or para-medic to avoid throwing the medicine away as had been the case with previous treatments. This treatment and supervision continued for from six months to two years during which time the patient was under regular observation.

Nurse Ruth Rodriques commented, "The results of this treatment have been 100% successful. In 1990 of the 4,192 patients on treatment 1,865 of them were declared healed. These remained under observation for a further five years to confirm their complete cure. The other 2,327 are currently on the MDT course even though some of these live in very remote areas. Our workers on the rivers travel constantly to treat them and to monitor their progress."

A report in the Rio Branco Gazeta highlighted the contribution made by these paramedics who travel so extensively:

Antonio Ademar Barahuna Bezerra, appropriately nicknamed "Courage," is the symbol of the fight against leprosy in Cruzeiro do Sul, the area worst effected by the disease in all the Acre State. For more than twenty-five years he has travelled by boat and canoe on all the rivers, streams and lakes of the Juruá Valley, from Ipixuna in Amazonas to the frontiers of Peru, sometimes walking for hours on forest trails, all this in pursuit of those afflicted with leprosy. He visits more than fifty thousand people each year looking for patients and taking the new treatment to those whom he discovers.

The programme to combat leprosy in the interior also covers the River Purus from the Peruvian borders to rapids below Boca do Acre in Amazonas as well as all the streams that flow into the Purus. Besides this there is work along the Rivers, Muru, Tarauaca, Juruá, Caete, Iaco, Envira, Tejo, Macaua, and Gregorio as well as among the people who live deep in the forest far from the rivers' edge.

In Cruzeiro do Sul, Courage and his helpers Elonita Soares and Paulo Martins diagnose and dispense medicines to all the new cases in the Juruá Valley. In Sena Madureira Democrito Costa Queiroz and Jose Natalicio cover the work on the River Purus and its tributaries. Another group look after the work in Tarauaca and the various rivers there. These are all dedicated workers who receive low wages, but with love and concern for the leprosy sufferers they work strenuously to help us eradicate the disease in our state.

For the success of this treatment it was necessary that Bill travel with the teams to these far distant centres to classify the patients, prescribe the medicine and where necessary, recommend some for surgery in Rio Branco. During most of 1988 and 1990 Bill travelled on thirty-five rivers which were upper tributaries of the great Amazon. The journeys lasted up to forty days.

After a short break in Rio Branco between these trips they were back on the rivers again. During those three years Bill spent each Christmas Day in a remote forest settlement with a tin of corned beef instead of the usual Christmas fare. Rations were meagre; discomforts were many, and insects, both flying and creeping, continually fed on Bill's good Ulster blood.

At night time they slept under palm leaf roofs; by day they sat in the canoe, sometimes through driving rain storms; at other times they swam across streams—all this to reach leprosy patients in remote areas. It may sound adventurous, but most people who visit the region will readily agree that after one day in the forest they have had enough. I assure you that days, weeks and months in these gruelling circumstances on the river and in the forest soon makes the so-called glamour disappear.

While Bill was gone on these trips Nurse Socorro, Dr. Leia and the rest of the team did a great job collecting the data sent in by the teams and kept careful records as the MDT programme demanded. Most of the Italian team continued their work in Cruzeiro do Sul.

When the two years were completed, thousands of patients had been classified and catalogued, but there was still a long back-log of operations to be done for patients who had been discovered in isolated regions during these trips. Dr. Silvano Renzo with Bill operated on many of these patients, and another newly qualified orthopaedic surgeon joined the team. Dr. Roberta Couto, a native of Rio Branco, showed great skills as a surgeon, and he had tremendous compassion for people. Working with Dr. Silvano Renzo greatly enhanced those skills, and soon a full weekly routine of reconstructive operations became her responsibility.

Chapter Twemty-Two

Body and Soul

❖

I n the towns visited and in Manaus and Rio Branco, Bill was
fully involved in the Lord's work. Missionaries and pastors in
the interior were glad to have him preach when he was available. He has encouraged, financially supported and counselled many
young pastors going into the work. For many years Bill was the
organist at the First Baptist Church of Rio Branco, which had been
established fifty years previously by the founder of the Acre Gospel
Mission, Mr. William McComb.

Pastor Elias Mendes, the pastor of the First Baptist Church, whose
wife Dr. Clara was a patient in the leprosy programme, remembers
the encouragement and support Bill always gave to them. He also
recalls Bill's fine sense of humour: "Not only was Bill our organist,
he was a great encouragement, and everyone enjoyed his preaching
and great sense of humour. His stories often lifted us or else had us
rolling in laughter. One night while Bill was at the organ and I was
leading the singing, I spied out of the corner of my eye Bill trying to
signal something to me. I wondered what he was trying to convey.
He continued to wave a finger in a given direction. Was the music

too slow? Was my tie not straight? His face was red, and he could hardly contain his laughter. I then saw why he had been signalling. Rats were running in and out from under the organ to the pulpit while we sang our heads off. By that time neither of us could sing for laughing, and as you can imagine, it was hard to preach following that."

Besides humour there were other qualities which Bill manifested, and yet in these very same qualities there were problems with which he struggled. In circumstances where there is such overwhelming need it must be matched with equal dedication and determination to do all possible to help. Yet, in this there are always dangers and pitfalls.

Great debate surrounds evangelical missionary activity in relation to the so called "social conscience." Often the missionary comes up against abject poverty and suffering. Has he a responsibility? As servants of Christ it is true that the emphasis should be on the spiritual man and not the physical. We labour for the eternal and not for the temporal—for the invisible and not the tangible. The social needs of a man are but the symptoms and result of his spiritual problem. In the light of all this, why treat the body? Why try to improve his living conditions?

Bill maintains what General William Booth, founder of the Salvation Army declared over a hundred years ago, "It is hard to preach the Gospel to a man when that man has an empty stomach." Booth did not preach a "social gospel." However, the Gospel of Jesus Christ is very practical and motivates Christians to help people in need. The model of our Lord, Who while on earth went about doing good, is our best example and highest motivation. Jesus Christ was not only interested in the ears to hear or the eyes to see but in the people and the whole person.

The leprous man of Matthew 8:1-4 was physically ill and ceremoniously unclean, and as a consequence he lived as a social outcast in sad isolation. Jesus bridged the social gap and touched him. He reversed the physical condition and healed him. The Saviour stimulated the man's spiritual perception, for the same leprous man was the first person of the New Testament to confess Jesus Christ as Lord.

Multiple cases of the Saviour's concern for the whole person, in sickness, in distress, in sorrow and bereavement, fill the pages of the Gospels. We do well to follow Him. It must also be stressed that beyond the dying body Bill Woods discerns the deeper, never dying soul. Beside the physical healing through his work Bill is glad the Good News of the Everlasting Gospel remedies the deeper malady of the human heart.

Another pitfall which can threaten a missionary involved in a caring ministry to suffering multitudes is evidenced when one's own spiritual devotion and vital communion with God are suffocated in the demands and busyness of an exacting programme. Bill is the first to admit that this is something with which he has battled so often and battles still. It is only too possible for the work to smother the worker's spiritual life. Ma Row in Bible School had often spoken of "the bareness of a busy life." Someone else had described service without corresponding spiritual devotion as "running on empty"—the engine is still running, but there is no petrol in the tank. Our Lord reminded us by the parable of the sheep that fell into the pit on the Sabbath, emergencies are not limited to six days in the week nor within the confines of a nine-to-five job. It has been difficult for Bill to keep that spiritual equilibrium.

To counterbalance this he is constantly reminded of our Lord who was so busy by day yet maintained the quiet times with His Father. Bill would not suggest this has been easy, nor has he always been as disciplined as he would like to have been. It is still something he tries to keep in balance. Priorities were never in conflict in the life of the Saviour, and He said, "Seek ye first the kingdom of God..."

The medical missionary often enjoys opportunities to minister to people at crucial and critical times in their lives. Sometimes to please the doctor or to extricate some extra benefit or favour from the medical staff, the patient mistakenly thinks that by professing conversion he will enhance his treatment or speed his cure. Genuine conversions are a joy to saints and angels. Spurious professions are a vexation to all. While discernment and wisdom are called for, Bill rests on the Scriptures that teach "the Lord knows those who are His."

With Bill's experience as a leprologist in remote and rural Brazil, his expertise was made use of in surveying and giving seminars in remote and underdeveloped areas of other countries. One of these was the former Portuguese colony of Angola. He had already been to Angola back in 1983, but in November 1990 Bill was invited to visit and survey the leprosy programme there. His fluent Portuguese and experience in the Amazon and elsewhere prompted the leprosy authorities in Brazil to send him to Luanda to conduct a seminar for the Angolan Ministry of Health and to be a delegate to their National Congress on Leprosy.

He was appalled with what he saw in that war torn country. His stay in Angola was short, and he was able to compare notes with some who were attempting a similar programme in that troubled African Republic. He visited the Kalukembe Hospital where before the war 20,000 leprosy patients were registered, and most of these had deformities resulting from their disease. Because of the war the number of registered cases had dropped to 4,000. Obviously many of these had either been killed in the war or scattered because of the war. Bill's survey challenged him greatly about the need of Africa and made him feel, "If only I could multiply my life and be able to serve in this continent also."

From Luanda, the capital, Bill's travels by plane and ambulance took him to southern Angola where the roads were littered with burned out tanks, machine gun riddled vehicles and other destroyed instruments of war. At times he became concerned for his own personal safety and especially when he heard that all regular flights back to Luanda were cancelled. The thought of being stranded in a war zone was not inviting.

Bill related what happened in a report he made of his trip:

On 22nd November, 1990 my travelling companion Dr. Antonio disappeared for the day. I was very happy to be on my own as for over a week I had been feeling unwell. I was glad to rest at the hotel that day. However, early the following morning we proceeded to the airport in an army ambulance. There was a change of plans, and we were taken to a Military Base instead of the civil airport as the general commercial flights had been cancelled. At the Military Base we spent the day waiting in the hope of being able to board a military flight back to Luanda.

At about 6:00 p.m. we felt it was pointless waiting any longer at the airport. I was very conscious that as an obvious foreigner I should not have been sitting for the whole day in a sensitive military area. Dr. Antonio kept assuring me there was no problem just as long as we stayed in the ambulance.

On 24th November we waited again all morning at the airport for possible transport to Luanda. Finally at 1:00 p.m. a large Russian military cargo plane with four jet turbines landed on the runway. By 5:00 p.m. the plane had been unloaded. At that point there was a mad stampede of about four hundred people all trying to board the aircraft. Those who were successful in their attempt were hastily ejected out of the front of the plane at a height of around ten feet. Soldiers tried to control the unruly mob. Finally, the Russians were allowed to board and some government officials. The ladder was then removed and the door shut. When the door was open again there was a lot of fighting. Soldiers tried to put people into a line, but the mob pushed and shouted until they were beaten back by the soldiers.

Dr. Antonio pushed me forward into this crowd. An angry soldier pushed me back out again. Another soldier rushed up and snatched my case and hurled it up unto the plane. The same soldier then pulled me through the bustling crowd, bent down and grabbed me around my legs and threw me up into the air. Whereupon a soldier, on his knees at the door of the aircraft, caught my arm and swung me back and forward until my legs came up high enough for yet another soldier to grab one leg, and both hauled me into the plane. I was finally on my way back to Luanda.

To say he made a speedy exit from Angola would be an understatement. From Angola he travelled on to the United Kingdom and to Belfast.

He had planned on staying only a week or so. The Lord had other plans. On arrival in Belfast he continued to feel feverish and unwell. A consultation with the doctor landed Bill in an isolation ward at the local Belvoir Park Hospital for Infectious Diseases—he had hepatitis. No wonder everybody thought he was a strange orange colour on returning from Africa. Those few weeks at home ran into a few months, and Bill had a forced but much needed rest. It was also an opportunity to spend Christmas with his sister.

When he finally returned to Brazil he was delighted to find that the administration work of the leprosy programme and the MDT treatment continued unabated. The computerisation of all of the data of patients, their treatment and their progress proved to be a big leap forward. The teams on the various rivers were reporting back their findings after weeks of travel on the river to supervise the treatment of their patients. Bill continued to work closely with Dr. Silvano Renzo and Dr. Roberta on the back-log of surgical cases who had come from interior towns.

During 1992-93 Bill travelled again throughout the interior of Acre to all the former places he had visited when he pioneered the MDT of patients who lived in the remotest parts of the forest. On this occasion the team took biopsies of the patients who had been on treatment to observe the effect of the MDT. Again these were long and arduous journeys often lasting for over a month at a time. The trips involved wading or swimming across streams, enduring a soaking in a rain storm or a scorching in the hot tropical sun, wading, at times, more than knee deep in mud and constantly watching for the ever dangerous snakes in the forest or alligators in the rivers. On and on the teams worked tirelessly until all the homes were visited again, biopsies taken and the data registered.

Bill related one incident:

At Christmas 1991 we travelled on the River Tarauac for fifteen days diagnosing and treating people as we went along. We then had to leave the boat and travel by canoe for another five days, sometimes pulling the loaded canoe over fallen trees or through the shallows. Finally we left the canoe and walked through the forest. Sometimes we were up to our knees in clay mud. At other times we waded through or swam across the streams.

Finally we came on a cluster of houses in a clearing where a man sat beside a lady with a child on her knee. The man had all the evident marks of leprosy, the deformed hands and feet and disfigured face. The woman asked, "Who are you?" I introduced myself and those with me and explained our purpose. The woman was dumbfounded. She told me she had been praying that the Lord would send some one to help her brother as they were too poor to go to Rio Branco. We were the answer to her prayer.

I looked at the man and explained that little could be done to recover his deformities. The lady spoke up and said it was not so much her brother she was worried about but her son. She did not want her son Josemir to become deformed like his uncle. Josemir emerged from inside the palm leaf covered jungle dwelling. He was a young boy of only twelve years. When we examined him, we discovered he already a had a tell-tale patch which indicated he had leprosy. We started him on treatment immediately. I assured them a para medic would call to visit them every three months. After two years of supervised treatment Josemir was finally declared leprosy free Christmas 1993 when we visited the area again. That was the best Christmas present he could ever have wished for.

In January 1997 I was on our boat again on the River Tarauaca at the very remote village of Jordao. A fine looking young man came on board. He looked at us as if we should recognise him. When we failed to identify who he was, he told us he was Josemir. He had just come to see me, for he wanted to say thank you. He had been completely cured.

In 1994 the Italian Programme was drawing to a close. The final statistics were taken to assess the effectiveness of the programme which had been initiated and directed by Bill and greatly helped and supported by his loyal team of workers in the capital and in the towns and on the rivers; the program was also greatly enhanced by the aid given by the Italians. The results were outstanding. In 1996 the incidence of leprosy in the Acre had fallen from eleven in every thousand inhabitants of the state to 1.5 patients in every thousand. The Acre Leprosy Programme under Dr. Bill Woods' leadership has become the most effective and efficient in all Brazil, and the former "Leprosy State" has been transformed to be a safer place to live where the prevalence of the dreaded disease has been greatly reduced.

According to Dr. Leia Borges when the statistics were presented at the Bauru Training Hospital at first they were met with some scepticism and questioning. It was thought that perhaps there was a mistake or someone could be exaggerating the figures. A specialist in the field was dispatched to the Acre to check out the statistics and verify the results. His visit confirmed all that had been declared on the assessment report which had previously been sent. Immediately the Acre leprosy project received great acclaim and recognition throughout Brazil.

At a World Congress on the Control of Leprosy held in Florida in August 1994 Bill was able to present a paper substantiated with a poster presentation showing that it was possible to administer MDT to people who live in the remotest regions providing there is a will to work and commitment to the job. Bill Woods and his dedicated team scattered throughout Acre were fine examples and proof of what he presented at that conference. The display made a great impression on leprosy authorities from all over the world, and the work was greatly commended by Dr. Noordeen, the Director of the Leprosy Department of the World Health Organisation.

Leprosy has not been eradicated in the Acre; however, it has been brought under manageable control. The difficult and tiresome journeys to remote areas still continue. Dr. Leia Borges said, "We have made big strides to get this far in our programme, but it is not the end. Our target is to reduce the incidence of leprosy to 0.1 people per thousand inhabitants of the Acre by the year 2000."

To achieve this goal, physical stamina and determined resolve are necessary for all the field workers, and Bill leads by example. Constant monitoring of the situation is necessary. Most, if not all, of the corrective operations for leprosy patients in Acre have been accomplished. The Italians withdrew from the programme apart from periodic donations and visits from their administrative consultants. With their departure Bill was sorry to lose a fine nurse and his virtual right hand, Socorro Brasiliense, who married one of the Italian team.

The orthopaedic surgeon Dr. Roberta suffered a set back when her new born baby developed meningitis almost immediately after birth, and she had to withdraw from the programme for a prolonged period. The old General Hospital in the centre of Rio Branco was fully renovated in 1995, and in the beautiful newly equipped building Bill's team was allocated a suite of consulting rooms for their out-patient clinic and administrative offices for the secretaries. Bill not only tastefully furnished these rooms at his own expense but also provided the modern ophthalmic equipment which had been purchased by gifts sent from friends in Northern Ireland.

Bill's expertise is now much sought after in other parts of Brazil and beyond. Invitations come regularly from many other Brazilian states requesting his counsel or inviting him to lead a seminar. Many of these states covet his presence for their local leprosy programmes. In the summer of 1997 the Minister of Health for Brazil, Dr. Abib Jatene, was in Rio Branco and paid an official visit to the Leprosy Unit at the hospital and publicly applauded the fine work the team has done. The Bolivian government's health department has solicited the services of Bill's Rio Branco team to train their workers in the technique of introducing the Multidrug Therapy to their frontier areas where they border with the Acre. Bill has been invited by the same government to give seminars in several large Bolivian cities.

Bill Woods has come a long way since the days of prescribing Californian Syrup of Figs and Scott's Emulsion for all ills and ailments. God has richly blessed His child, gifted him, guided him and protected him. In those times when Bill was hurting through frustrated plans, shattered dreams and a broken heart, God comforted him, and later thousands of people in Brazil would rise up to call him blessed.

Nurse Ruth Rodriques says, "The patients say that under God in heaven Dr. Bill is their father. He is dedicated and untiring in his work for his patients. We thank God for Dr. Bill."

His close co-worker Dr. Leia Borges says:

I cannot find words to describe the work of this man. He is so human and down to earth, and yet he is so dedicated and resolute in his drive to help his patients.

He is greatly respected by all his professional colleagues, and throughout the state everybody from the state governor, senators, members of parliament, council members of Rio Branco and council members of each small town to the porters at the hospital all acclaim the work he has done. What they don't understand is why he should come from his own country, sacrifice so much professionally and submit himself to such deprivation at times to help those who people perceive to be the poorest people of our society. Often he subsidises the purchase of their medicines or pays their travel to and from the interior towns. All of us in the team thank God for giving us a leader who is not only kind and considerate but has set a great example to us all.

Unaffected, Bill is spontaneous and genuine in combining his social concern and surgical skills with his love for souls and dedication to his Lord. Undoubtedly, the attention he gives to the dying body is because of his compassion for the never-dying souls of his patients.

To all of his colleagues in the Acre Gospel Mission Bill's devoted life, his single-minded purpose, selfless sacrifice and service have been both a challenge and an inspiration to all. We have been privileged to watch God's hand shaping His servant from the first day he courageously stepped out on this venture of faith. The world may pour its terms of "humanitarian" and "philanthropist" on such a person. "A servant of Jesus Christ" is what Bill Woods wanted to be when he surrendered his life to the Saviour forty years ago. He still simply lives for the day when he will hear, "Well done good and faithful servant."

One day recently Bill dropped Audrey and me off at the airport at Rio Branco for a planned visit to Tarauaca. Before he left he introduced us to two of his leprosy patients on whom he and Dr. Roberta had recently performed some orthopaedic surgery to straighten feet that had been deformed because of their disease. After four operations and many physiotherapy sessions spread over three months they were now returning home. Both were wearing special orthopaedic leather sandals manufactured at Ursula's local workshop and were fully cured from leprosy after two years of the MDT treatment. They were now returning to their families as new men.

While still in the airport departure lounge one of the patients came over to speak to us. Raimundo at twenty-nine years of age was already a widower. His young wife of twenty-five years had died very suddenly leaving him with two sons, five and six years old. He enquired if we were related to Dr. Bill. When we told him we were his colleagues, he began to tell us how Dr. Bill had found him, diagnosed his disease, put him on treatment and then arranged to fly him and his cousin, who was also a patient, over to Rio Branco where both had foot surgery. As he told us of the care and attention Bill had shown him, a lump came to his throat and he began to cry. He said he could never thank God enough for what Bill had done for him. Bill had not only operated on his feet but literally had put Raimundo back on his feet and given him new hope for the future and the ability to work to help sustain his two children. Beside all this, Bill had given each of the young men a copy of the Scriptures and encouraged them to read the Gospel.

In November 1996 I boarded a small twin engine plane for the half hour flight from the Amazon town of Boca do Acre to Rio Branco. As I mounted the few steps there was only one passenger already on board—an older, obviously very poor man with only one crutch. The peak of his baseball cap was pulled down over his face to hide his features. We exchanged some casual greetings, and I made my way to a seat in front of him. I secured my seat belt, and soon we were climbing up into the clouds that drifted above the familiar green jungle.

A few minutes into the flight the old man behind me reached over and touched my shoulder. I looked around, and although the cap still shadowed most of his face, I could see by the drooping cheeks that hung like empty sacks and his hairless eye-brows, he suffered from leprosy. He focused his beady eyes on me and then asked, "Are you Pastor Victor?"

Surprised by the question I answered in the affirmative. His tooth-less grin seemed to fill up the empty cheeks, and a gleam was in his eye as he lifted the cap. "Geraldo!" I exclaimed. "Are you Geraldo from Labrea?"

He nodded his head affirming his identity. This was the first leprosy patient Bill had ever met thirty-six years previously, and he had introduced him to us the first weekend we arrived in Labrea in 1965.

"What are you doing here? Where are you going?" I quizzed.

"I am going to Rio Branco. Dr Bill is going to operate on my eyes," he answered.

"Does Bill know you are coming?" I enquired further.

"No." was his short answer. "He operated on my legs and hands; now he will give me my full sight back again."

Bill met us at the airport and made arrangements for Geraldo to be taken to hospital by ambulance. Before he left he said to me, "The next time we meet I'll see you better." He was obviously anticipating his operation.

We later learned that while waiting for surgery at Rio Branco, Geraldo, at seventy-one years of age, after a short illness, went to be with his Lord. He had always lived in the hope of his body being repaired and the eyesight restored. Now for him the suffering is forever gone, and his corrupt and perishing body has been transformed and made like unto Christ's glorious body.

Chapter Twenty-Three

All the Way

❖

Those who read this story should not be fooled into thinking that it is a tale of sensational adventure or stupendous success. On the contrary. Bill's life has been one of difficulty, heartache, and often times tears have accompanied the blessings God has sent. The goals that Dr. Woods has reached were not obtained without following the Biblical way that Bill learned when he was yet a student in Glasgow.

The way of faith. The first step of faith at conversion was only the beginning in what has been a life of faith—faith in God to guide in sunshine and in the dark, to provide in hours of need, faith to face impossibilities, faith to trust in times of sorrow and hurt when the human hand could not trace the way ahead and the natural eye could not see, faith to accomplish all that God had planned for him.

Discouragement can often cause our faith to shrink, and adversity can lead us to despair. As an example of this remember the disciples of our Lord in the storm on Galilee. One of the characteristics of mature faith is the ability to endure—even in the face of adversity and discouragement. Bill had to learn to walk by faith and not by sight, and in that walk he learned to prove that faith which is never tested is a faith that never developes.

Warren Weirsbie says, "Living by faith is trusting God without scheming." When Bill stepped out on this great venture he did so on the basis of a promise God gave him, "For the vision is yet for an appointed time, but at the end it shall speak, and not lie: though it tarry, wait for it; because it will surely come, it will not tarry. Behold, his soul which is lifted up is not upright in him: but the just shall live by his faith." (Habakuk 2:3,4) Bill learned to live and walk by faith as God instructed in this promise. He has also worked in faith and love. Although Bill did not always see the easy and early results of his work, he learned to leave the outcome in the hands of His Heavenly Father. Bill found that faith is simply resting on Jehovah's faithfulness for He never denies Himself.

The way of sacrifice. For all who follow Christ, the divine altar of self sacrifice is waiting. What do we place on that altar? The Saviour taught Bill and calls us all to sacrifice our will, surrender our ways and place our steps in the footprints of the Saviour to follow Him. Multitudes have benefited from Dr. Woods' unstinting generosity, and some day, the full extent of Bill's work will be known, and thousands will rise up to praise the Lamb because Bill Woods gave his life as a living sacrifice to God to prove what was the good, perfect and acceptable will of God in his life. He has been able to grasp rich gems for the Almighty simply because he was prepared to let go his grip on the cheaper toys of life even though at times they had to be pried out of his grasp.

The way of obedience. From the day he stepped out from home and employment to go into training, Bill recognised "there is no other way but to trust and obey." It has not always been easy to obey. Often it has meant a lonely path which was different from the direction that others were taking and one which was misunderstood by some. A close relationship with the Lord has not always been easy in the rush and scramble of a busy programme nor in the darker and difficult periods of life. However, he did discover that in order to be led in the right paths, one not only needs to be sensitive the Shepherd's voice, but also willing to submit to the Shepherd's plan and follow wherever He might lead.

The way of fellowship. You will admit, having read this book, that it has been a somewhat lonely life, and yet the truth is Bill has never been alone. The Lord promised never to leave us as orphans. Besides the constant presence of the Saviour, Bill has been blessed by many friends and colleagues who have buoyed him up with their letters, encouraged him with their support, strengthened him with their prayers and now rejoice with Him to see all the Lord has done through this one yielded life.

In Brazil Bill and his team of workers have received many accolades for the work they have done. In August 1981 the City Council of Cruzeiro do Sul made Bill an honorary citizen of their municipality. Likewise, in November 1990 the City Council of Rio Branco conferred an honorary citizenship to Bill.

At the Congress for Leprosy in Endemic Countries, convened at the famous Iguaco Falls on 5th June 1997, the Brazilian College of Dermatologists conferred an honorary award on Bill in recognition of his excellent work in Acre.

On 28th May 1993 and again on 3rd June 1997 the Brazilian senator Flaviano Flavio de Melo made speeches in the Brazilian Senate acknowledging the benefit and blessing Dr. William John Woods and his team have been to thousands of Brazilians who were victims of what used to be termed an incurable disease. By his dedicated life and service Bill had brought relief and new hope to many.

In addressing the Senate Sr. Flaviano said:

It is worth calling your attention to the fact that the most stirring work being done to combat leprosy in Acre began in 1979 with the arrival of Dr. William John Woods. He diagnosed and organised files on all the patients, set up permanent teams to administer and monitor treatment in all the interior towns in Acre.

Today that team in the Acre Dermatology and Hygiene Department, which some years ago numbered twelve people, is now composed of 140 workers. All of these are committed to combating leprosy in our vast region.

Mr. President and fellow senators, much and all as we speak of these people, it is difficult for us to have any real idea what is involved in this work and how difficult it is to carry it out. This work is not done primarily in hospitals nor clinics as you might imagine.

On the contrary, the greater part of this service is done in the jungle, in extremely distant and isolated places. These are places where access is not only difficult, but those who venture to these areas do so only either out of personal necessity or dedicated love, and it is this sort of love and dedication that motivates Dr. Woods and his team.

Many of these workers, including Dr. William John Woods, trek constantly in the forest where they normally spend twenty to thirty days travelling in canoes, on animals or on foot. They face tropical downpours, raging floods, malaria carrying mosquitoes, poisonous snakes and all the adverse conditions that life in the jungle imposes on them. All this they do to search out and treat those who are afflicted with this dreaded disease called leprosy.

On 1st January 1997, Dr. Bill's work was recognised by her Majesty Queen Elizabeth II who awarded him an OBE (Official of the Order of the British Empire). An invitation was given, or better still, a summons was issued, to receive the award at Buckingham Palace. The date for that award has been set for 4th November 1997, and Bill's sister Nina and brothers Bob and Alex plan to be present.

Typical of Bill's modesty, and perhaps more importantly his sense of priority, when he was congratulated on receiving the award he commented, "I very much appreciate the award but would prefer to hear my Heavenly Father say, 'Well done thou good and faithful servant.'" For all who serve our Lord, that day is yet to come.

A Layman looks at Leprosy

❖
——————————— ❖ ———————————

"PRINCESS BRINGS ROYAL TOUCH TO LEPROSY CAM-PAIGN" So read the bold headline carried by Britain's Daily Telegraph on 9th December, 1996. Diana, Princess of Wales, was addressing the 30th anniversary of the International Federation of Anti-Leprosy Associations in central London. During the course of her speech she said, "Leprosy is not something of the past. It has not disappeared from the list of medical diseases. Last year more than 500,000 new cases were detected."

It is true that Leprosy is one of the oldest scourges of mankind, but it is also estimated by the World Health Organisation that there are more than twelve million people who suffer from the disease throughout the world today. This chronic infectious disease is most prevalent in tropical countries but not necessarily related to the climate. Leprosy also exists in colder climates. It generally affects the peripheral nerves and the skin, although it can also impact other systems of the body.

Contrary to popular opinion leprosy is only mildly contagious, and prolonged close contact is usually considered to be necessary for the disease to be transmitted. However, although 95% of the population will never contract leprosy, it is also true that there are some people who are predisposed and susceptible to the disease, and even casual or short term contact will result in transmission of the leprosy bacilli. The incubation period for the disease is generally thought to be anything from three months to forty years with an average of about five years.

It is probable that African slaves imported leprosy to the Americas in the sixteenth century. Today Brazil has the greatest number of leprosy sufferers in South America, and before Bill Woods' leprosy programme got under way, the state of Acre had the highest incidence of the disease per ratio of population in all national territories.

Depending on the degree of a patient's resistance to the disease leprosy presents a wide spectrum of features ranging from small isolated hazy discoloured patches to widespread and multiple shiny raised nodules and any intermediate stage between the two. It generally presents a loss of sensation in an affected area, or even an acute form can result in a sudden paralysis where a motor nerve has been affected.

It is this loss of sensation that leaves the patient vulnerable by not being able to discriminate between hot and cold or to recognise pain. This often results in burns and damage to the hands and feet. Leprosy does not destroy the limbs--the destruction and deformity of the body's members is a secondary effect of the disease. A healthy person feels pain due to injury from thorns, nails, cuts, burns, heat, etc., and therefore takes care to protect his limbs. However, patients with leprosy continue to use their hands and feet when they can no longer feel pain. It is the resulting lack of sensation that causes the patient to repeatedly injure his body, and over a prolonged period of time, when the limbs are not cared for, the patient will lose toes, fingers and even his limbs.

Likewise where motor nerves are involved on the face, the patient will lose the normal use of the eyelids resulting in scar tissues on the cornea and eventual blindness. Damage to ulnar or median nerves on the arms results in impairment of finger movement which leads to wrist-drop and claw hammer hands. Damage to nerves behind the knee and on the lower leg often produce a drop-foot whereby the patient either trails his foot or is forced to lift his leg high enough to compensate for the drop-foot. These are all secondary deformities which result from damaged nerves.

Some primary features of leprosy may be observed in the loss of eye brows and eye lashes, cauliflower-ears, flattened nose and dry skin (due to lack of sweating).

Because of the fear, shame and social stigma associated with the disease, leprosy is greatly unreported and often times misrepresented or misunderstood. Even, at times, statistics are suppressed so that the true incidence of leprosy is not revealed nor the exact number of patients known. The disease is sometimes referred to as "Hansen's Disease" in respect to the bacteriologist who first separated the leprosy bacilli.

Since missionary Dr. R. G. Cochrane discovered the beneficial use of Dapsone in 1946, the chemotherapy treatment of leprosy has come a long way and given hope to patients. Today, providing a patient can be diagnosed early enough, great results are possible with the new Multidrug Treatment (MDT). However, the treatment of leprosy goes far beyond the chemotherapy of MDT. Reconstructive surgery is needed when it is possible to restore the use of limbs, and ophthalmic surgery to restore sight to those whose corneas have been made obscure with scar tissue. Besides all this, the leprosy patient needs moral support and reassurance so that he can gain self respect and confidence in a society where in previous generations those who suffered from the illness were isolated from the normal world.

The American Leprosy Mission states the following:

Humanity's fear of leprosy is, for the patient, one of the worst effects of the disease. Rooted in the myths of history and pre-history, that fear often isolates the afflicted person. Marriages break up from fear of infection; jobs are lost; some communities force infected persons away from their homes; some schools and hospitals deny patients admission to their precincts.

Many who have leprosy subconsciously believe the old myths. Such beliefs, combined with a stricken person's natural dismay over visible physical changes that stem from untreated leprosy, shatter self esteem. The individual begins to feel worthless and unclean. The old myths stem from fear engendered by the supposed incurability of Hansen's disease. The myth's include:

Belief that leprosy is an evidence of personal sin. Belief that leprosy is a punishment given by God. Belief that leprosy is communicable to everyone. Belief that disabilities inevitably occur in leprosy.

It is reported that the Princess of Wales has visited anti-leprosy projects all over the world. In touching and hugging leprosy patients, she has done much to remove the stigma attached to the disease. The British newspaper The Daily Telegraph quoted her as saying, "It has always been my concern to touch people with leprosy—trying to show in a simple action that they are not reviled nor are we repulsed."

Bill Woods ministry to the sufferers of leprosy has not been to just touch and treat the body alone, but it has also been to bring the Master's touch to the whole person, relief and healing to the body and pardon and peace to the never dying soul. Through the various teams he has organised in the interior towns of the Acre the most remote homes have been visited to register those who suffer from Hansen's disease. The new MDT has been made available to them all, and return journeys are made over a period of two years to supervise the progress of the treatment. Hundreds have been certified as healed from the disease and discharged.

His surgical skills and those of his colleagues have also been employed in reconstructive and ophthalmic surgery restoring mobility to previously impaired limbs and returning sight to those blinded as a result of their illness.

Through physiotherapy and rehabilitation, reassurance and self-respect have been imparted to many, and they can now find a place in the normal world. More important still, through the Gospel of Jesus Christ, Bill Woods has introduced the deeper and more eternal dimension of showing the way of salvation through Jesus Christ alone.

Leprosy and the Bible

❖

T he American Leprosy Mission in its public exhibit at the Greenville, South Carolina headquarters in the United States provide some excellent clarification of Hansen's disease and the ancient world.

Leprosy in the Ancient World

Humanity's response to leprosy has always fallen to two poles.

At one extreme we have sought to identify, isolate condemn and punish the person with leprosy.

At the other extreme, some have tried to serve and save those stricken by the disease. Meanwhile, physicians of every age have sought to describe, explain and defeat the illness. The ancient world was no exception. Rameses II of Egypt, in 1300 B.C. took pride in the fact that people with leprosy who used his waterwells seemed to be healed. Phoenicians of 1500 B.C. attributed leprosy to the god Bes (Xensu to the Egyptians), who was depicted on pottery as

having leprosy. Some Egyptian legends explained the exodus of the
Hebrews as an expulsion made necessary by the presence of leprosy
among them.

Leprsoy is mentioned as a curse in Shinto prayers of 1250 B.C.
in Japan.

The Marquis of Yun (750 B.C.) a friend of Confucius, had leprosy. Confucius, unlike others of his day, found it a mystery rather
than evidence of divine displeasure. We can seldom be altogether
sure that the diseases mentioned or pictured in ancient manuscripts
or artefacts were indeed leprosy. Sometimes, we now know, they
were not.

Leprosy in The Old Testament

In ancient Israel, the priest was the only physician. He was
charged not only with treating sickness but also with protecting the
temple against ritual uncleanness.

One of the diseases thought to be both illness and an evidence of
ritual uncleanness was tsara-ath, a condition associated with blemishes of the skin and with physical imperfections. The word tsara-
ath also was used to describe blemishes on cloth, leather and buildings.

The ancient Greeks called leprosy elephatiasis, employing a different word, lepra, for another set of scaly skin diseases. Translators who rendered the Septuagint (Greek) version of the Old Testament, in 200 B.C., translated tsara-ath as lepra. Later, Latin translators working from the Greek and other texts wrongly understood
lepra to mean the disease now called leprosy, or Hansen's disease,
and subsequent translators into modern languages repeated the
error. Modern medical scientists now know that many of the
descriptions of leprosy in Old Testament Scriptures refer to other
disorders.

In fact, the Old Testament does not always relate tsara-ath to
uncleanness or to sin. Though King Uzziah contracted tsara-ath as
punishment for sin (2 Chron. 26:21), Moses in a celebrated passage
was given tsara-ath as a sign of God's presence (Ex.4:6).

Jesus and Leprosy

In New Testament times leprosy was well known in the Middle East and was no doubt accurately diagnosed by the Greek-trained physician Dr. Luke who wrote the third gospel.

New Testament references to leprosy are in the context of healing, restoration, and social well-being. Jesus knew that leprosy and other afflictions were not caused by sin or by God's disfavour (Luke 13:4), so He was not disgusted or repelled by people who had the disease. In the main stories about Jesus healing people, He made no distinction between the victims of leprosy and of other afflictions. (Matt 8:2-16; 9:1-8; 9:27-33) Jesus willingly touched leprosy patients and at least on one occasion went for dinner at the home of a leper. While Jesus lived, however, the general society continued to treat people with leprosy with great severity. The Old Testament prohibitions mentioned in Leviticus were at the base of common attitudes. "And the leper in whom the plague is, his clothes shall be rent, and his head bare, and he shall put a covering upon his upper lip, and shall cry, 'Unclean, unclean, unclean.' All the days wherein the plague shall be in him he shall be defiled; he is unclean: he shall dwell alone; without the camp shall his habitation be." Leviticus 13:45,46

"Command the children of Israel, that they put out of the camp every leper, and everyone that hath an issue, and whosoever is defiled by the dead: both male and female shall ye put out, without the camp shall ye put them; that they defile not their camps, in the midst whereof I dwell." Numbers 5:2,3

Immediately after the Sermon on the Mount Jesus descended to where the needy sought Him, and He was worshipped by a man who had leprosy. This man was the first person in the New Testament to call Jesus Christ "Lord". Is it any wonder the Saviour stretched forth His hand and touched him?